THIS BOOK BELONGS TO

_____

START DATE

_____

SHE READS TRUTH

EXECUTIVE

FOUNDER/CHIEF EXECUTIVE OFFICER
Raechel Myers

CO-FOUNDER/CHIEF CONTENT OFFICER
Amanda Bible Williams

CHIEF OPERATING OFFICER
Ryan Myers

EXECUTIVE ASSISTANT
Catherine Cromer

EDITORIAL

CONTENT DIRECTOR
John Greco, MDiv

MANAGING EDITOR
Jessica Lamb

PRODUCT MANAGER, KIDS READ TRUTH
Melanie Rainer, MATS

CONTENT EDITOR
Kara Gause

ASSOCIATE EDITORS
Bailey Gillespie
Ellen Taylor

CREATIVE

CREATIVE DIRECTOR
Jeremy Mitchell

LEAD DESIGNER
Kelsea Allen

ARTIST IN RESIDENCE
Emily Knapp

DESIGNERS
Abbey Benson
Davis DeLisi

MARKETING

MARKETING DIRECTOR
Casey Campbell

MARKETING MANAGER
Katie Matuska

SOCIAL MEDIA STRATEGIST
Ansley Rushing

PARTNERSHIP SPECIALIST
Kamiren Passavanti

COMMUNITY SUPPORT SPECIALIST
Margot Williams

SHIPPING & LOGISTICS

LOGISTICS MANAGER
Lauren Gloyne

SHIPPING MANAGER
Sydney Bess

FULFILLMENT COORDINATOR
Katy McKnight

FULFILLMENT SPECIALISTS
Sam Campos
Julia Rogers

SUBSCRIPTION INQUIRIES
orders@shereadstruth.com

@SHEREADSTRUTH

Download the
She Reads Truth app,
available for iOS
and Android.

SHEREADSTRUTH.COM

This book was printed offset in Nashville, Tennessee, on 70# Lynx Opaque. Cover is 100# Cougar Opaque with a soft touch lamination.

1 & 2 KINGS

OUR GOD REIGNS

King Jesus has come and
is coming again, and His
kingdom will never end, just
as God promised David.

John Greco
CONTENT DIRECTOR

The Aramean commander Naaman came to Israel when he heard there was a prophet in the land who could heal him of his skin disease. He was healed and returned home knowing that the blessings given to Israel were from the Lord (2Kg 5:15). In that short episode, the nation God set apart as His own lived up to its calling—to be "a light to the nations," as Isaiah would later put it (Is 42:6). But sadly, this was only a glimpse into what could have been.

First and 2 Kings record the tragic history of God's people, from the twilight of David's reign to the long march into exile. Rather than being a light to the nations of the world, the divided kingdoms of Israel and Judah were more often fellow participants in the dark practices of the nations' gods. In the northern kingdom of Israel, it seems each successive king tried to outdo the evil of his predecessor. And in the southern kingdom of Judah, things were only marginally better. Notable exceptions like Hezekiah and Josiah walked in the ways of David, but most of the kings failed to live up to the standards set by God.

Despite the tapestry of wickedness, sewn together with squares of violence and idolatry, there is a thread of faithfulness winding its way through the complicated story of the two nations: God keeps His promises. King Jesus has come and is coming again, and His kingdom will never end, just as God promised David. And He has indeed blessed all the nations of the earth, just as God promised Abraham. He is the light of the world (Jn 8:12). No government or ruler, no matter how abhorrent, has the power to overturn God on this matter.

For readers of 1 and 2 Kings today, this message can get lost among the unfamiliar people, places, and plotlines. For that reason, we've included some helpful extras in this four-week reading plan. First, there's a "Setting the Stage" section that places 1 and 2 Kings into the larger story of Scripture (p. 14). Next, there's an illustration of Solomon's temple (p. 40) and a roundup of Israel's neighbors (p. 64). There's a timeline of the kings of Israel and Judah (p. 138), as well as a chart that shows how Elisha's ministry foreshadowed the life of Jesus (p. 168). Every mention of God remembering His covenant with David is also highlighted in gold.

When Naaman left Israel, he took dirt with him back to Aram so he could worship on ground that belonged to the Lord. My prayer is that as you read 1 and 2 Kings, you will be drawn into worship of the King of kings, knowing that wherever you set your feet, our God reigns.

ABCDEFGHIJKLMN
OPQRSTUVWXYZ
0123456789

At that time Solomon assembled the elders of Israel,
all the tribal heads and the ancestral leaders of the
Israelites before him at Jerusalem in order to bring
the ark of the Lord's covenant from the city of David,
that is Zion. So all the men of Israel were assembled
in the presence of King Solomon in the month of
Ethanim, which is the seventh month, at the festival.

PANTONE®
1245 U

PANTONE®
705 U

PANTONE®
538 U

DESIGN ON PURPOSE

Kintsugi is the Japanese art of repairing broken pottery using
lacquer mixed with powdered gold to highlight and dignify
the object's history. The use of kintsugi throughout this book
celebrates God's faithfulness and reflects His redemption of
humanity's brokenness. The photography tells the story of this
process—a picture of how broken pieces can be mended to
create a restored and beautiful whole.

Our artist in residence created the kintsugi-inspired lines that appear on select spreads, visual representations of God's devotion to His covenant with David.

She Reads Truth is a community of women dedicated to reading the Word of God every day.

The Bible is living and active, breathed out by God, and we confidently hold it higher than anything we can do or say. This book focuses primarily on Scripture, with bonus resources to facilitate deeper engagement with God's Word.

At the start of each daily reading, you'll find these icons indicating which kings and kingdom are covered in the day's text.

References to the Davidic covenant are marked in gold in the daily readings (see page 19).

People and deities marked in **bold** are included the "Neighbors of Israel and Judah" extra on pages 64–67.

SCRIPTURE READING

Designed for a Monday start, this Study Book presents the books of 1 and 2 Kings in daily readings, with supplemental passages for additional context.

JOURNALING SPACE

Each weekday features space for personal reflection and prayer.

GRACE DAY

Use Saturdays to pray, rest, and reflect on what you've read.

WEEKLY TRUTH

Sundays are set aside for weekly Scripture memorization.

Find the corresponding memory cards in the back of this book.

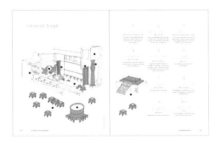

EXTRAS

This book features additional tools to help you gain a deeper understanding of the text.

1 & 2 Kings

4 Weeks

PLAN OVERVIEW

After centuries of conquest and struggle, King David united the twelve tribes of Israel into a single kingdom and led them into a golden era as a nation. The narrative of 1 and 2 Kings recounts what happened over the next four hundred years: from the prosperity of Solomon's reign, to civil war and exile, from the construction of the temple to the worship of other gods. Along the way, wicked kings led Israel and Judah further away from the Lord, while God's prophets called them back to the truth.

For added community and conversation, join us in the **1 & 2 Kings** reading plan on the She Reads Truth app or at SheReadsTruth.com.

TABLE OF CONTENTS

WEEK

WEEK

WEEK

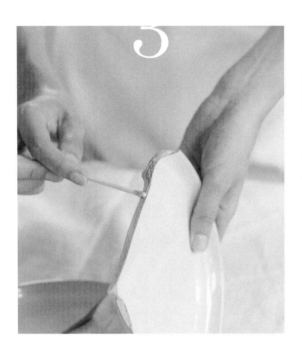

3

WEEK

4

EXTRAS

Introduction

On the Timeline

The history recorded in 1 and 2 Kings covers approximately 400 years. It begins around 970 BC with the death of King David, and ends around 560 BC with the release of King Jehoiachin from prison in Babylon. In 931 BC, the nation of Israel split into two kingdoms. Later both kingdoms went into exile (Israel in 722 BC and Judah in 586 BC).

A Little Background

First and 2 Kings are the history of the kings and kingdoms of Israel and Judah. Originally, the two were one book, but they were later divided by the translators of the Septuagint (the Greek translation of the Old Testament).

The Davidic covenant (first introduced in 2 Samuel) established the king as the moral representative of the people for covenant purposes. Covenant blessings were given or withheld on the basis of the king's behavior, making the behavior of the king the basis of covenant faithfulness for any given reign.

Message & Purpose

The theological perspective of 1 and 2 Kings is expressed in a number of themes:

- The sinfulness of the kings and the nation
- The conflict between the demands of practical politics and the demands of faith
- The glory God gave to the obedient covenant kings
- God's harshness in judgment on some occasions and leniency on others
- The conflict between the worship of the Lord and the worship of other gods

Give Thanks for the Books of 1 and 2 Kings

For the Bible writers, history could not have existed without God's purposes, thereby making all history theological. The Babylonian exiles wanted an explanation for what they saw as the failure of the religious system in Israel, so they looked to historical apologetics to find their answers. The books of 1 and 2 Kings interpreted Hebrew history in light of Old Testament covenant theology, finding the "failure" was due not to God, but to God's people who did not uphold their part of the covenant. God is faithful to His covenant with us, even when we are not.

The books of 1 and 2 Kings are part of the Old Testament story of Israel, the nation set apart by God to bless the world. That story can be summarized in three parts:

1

THE PATRIARCHS

God called Abraham to leave his home and follow Him to the land of Canaan. He made a covenant with Abraham to make him the father of a great nation, give him Canaan as an inheritance, and bless the world through his offspring. Abraham's grandson Jacob, also called Israel, had twelve sons, whose descendants established the twelve tribes of Israel.

2

THE EXODUS AND THE LAW

God used Moses to bring the Israelites out of slavery in Egypt. At Mount Sinai, God made a covenant with Israel, setting them apart as His people in order to make His name known among the nations. He also gave them the Law, the standard by which they were to live and worship.

3

THE NATION OF ISRAEL

Under Joshua, the Israelites entered the promised land and began to displace the people living there. When Joshua died, the people turned from God. Their sin led to cycles of judgment and deliverance. Eventually, the people cried out for a king, and God gave them Saul as the first king of Israel. Saul was followed by David, then David's son Solomon. After Solomon's reign, the nation divided. Parallel lines of mostly wicked kings ruled the two kingdoms until Israel, the northern kingdom, and Judah, the southern kingdom, were taken into captivity by foreign powers. After seventy years, groups of exiles from Judah began to return to Israel and rebuild.

Appointing
a King

·
·
·

In Deuteronomy 17, before the Israelites crossed
the Jordan River to claim the promised land, God
established a standard for how Israel's future kings
were to set themselves apart from the kings of
neighboring communities. As you read about the
reigns recorded in 1 and 2 Kings, reflect on how the
various rulers failed to obey God's instruction.

" . . . so that he may learn to fear the LORD his God, to observe all the words of this instruction, and to do these statutes."

"When you enter the land the LORD your God is giving you, take possession of it, live in it, and say, 'I will set a king over me like all the nations around me,' you are to appoint over you the king the LORD your God chooses. Appoint a king from your brothers. You are not to set a foreigner over you, or one who is not of your people. However, he must not acquire many horses for himself or send the people back to Egypt to acquire many horses, for the LORD has told you, 'You are never to go back that way again.' He must not acquire many wives for himself so that his heart won't go astray. He must not acquire very large amounts of silver and gold for himself. When he is seated on his royal throne, he is to write a copy of this instruction for himself on a scroll in the presence of the Levitical priests. It is to remain with him, and he is to read from it all the days of his life, so that he may learn to fear the LORD his God, to observe all the words of this instruction, and to do these statutes. Then his heart will not be exalted above his countrymen, he will not turn from this command to the right or the left, and he and his sons will continue reigning many years in Israel."

3

The Davidic Covenant

When David wanted to make a house for God in Jerusalem, God responded by saying He would make a house for David—a royal line that would never come to an end (2Sm 7:13, 16). Each subsequent king was called to follow after David by keeping the statutes and commands of God. Time and time again, God remembered His promise and kept David's royal line intact through the reigns of kings who failed to follow David's example. Though the monarchy came to an end when the people of Judah were taken into exile by the Babylonians, God's promise remained. During this exile, the prophets continued to speak of a coming Messiah, an "anointed one" from the branch of David who would reign as a righteous King without end (Is 9:6–7).

He is the one who will build a house for my name, and I will establish the throne of his kingdom forever.

2 SAMUEL 7:13

The New Testament writers celebrate Jesus Christ as this anticipated Messiah—the divine Son of God, heir to David's throne, and the one who reigns forever and ever. As you read 1 and 2 Kings, take note of the gold text that appears in the daily readings. Each instance is a reminder of God's covenant with David and His promise of Jesus, the Messiah.

. . .

4

Claims to David's Throne

.
.
.

Beginning just a few years after the events that occur at the close of 2 Samuel, the opening chapters of 1 Kings describe the final days of King David's life and the start of King Solomon's reign. These chapters read like a sequel, where the author assumes the reader is familiar with the people and events of 1 and 2 Samuel. On the following page you'll find background information on the key players in the political rivalry that unfolds at the beginning of 1 Kings.

King David

Replaced King Saul as God's chosen king; ruled for forty years. David was a shepherd, warrior, musician, and a man after God's own heart (1Sm 16–17). God made a covenant with David, promising that He would establish an eternal kingdom through David's line (2Sm 7).

DAVID'S SONS

Adonijah

David's fourth son (2Sm 3:4). At the end of David's life, Adonijah was the king's eldest living son and attempted to claim David's throne.

Absalom

David's third son (2Sm 3:3). An attractive and charismatic leader, Absalom was killed when he attempted to overthrow David (2Sm 13–18).

Solomon

David's son whom "the LORD loved" (2Sm 12:24). David chose Solomon to be the successor to his throne and the one through whom God's covenant promise would continue.

ADONIJAH'S SUPPORTERS

Joab

David's nephew and the commander of David's army (2Sm 8:16; 20:23). During a time of peace, Joab killed Abner, the commander of Saul's army, and Amasa, one of his personal rivals (2Sm 2:18–23; 20:9–10).

Abiathar

One of the high priests during David's reign and an early supporter of David (1Sm 22:20–22).

SOLOMON'S SUPPORTERS

Nathan

A prophet who advised David throughout his reign and delivered God's covenant to David (2Sm 7).

Bathsheba

The widow of Uriah and one of David's many wives (2Sm 11). After her first son with David died, Bathsheba gave birth to Solomon (2Sm 12:15–25).

Zadok

A priest who served alongside Abiathar during David's reign (2Sm 8:17).

Benaiah

A commander of David's bodyguard and an honored member of David's mighty warriors (2Sm 20:23; 23:20–23).

David's royal guard

Also known as David's mighty warriors, this group of men supported David when he lived in hiding from Saul before David became king (2Sm 21:15–22; 23:8–39).

1 KINGS

When all the people saw it, they fell facedown and said,
"The Lord, he is God! The Lord, he is God!"

1 KINGS 18:39

Final Days of King David
1KG 1–2

.
.
.

Adonijah tries to seize the throne
1:1–40

Solomon anointed as David's successor
1:41–53

David's charge to Solomon
2:1–12

Solomon's Reign over the United Kingdom
1KG 2–11

.
.
.

Solomon deals with his opponents
2:13–46

Solomon's wisdom
3:1–28

Solomon's officials
4:1–19

Solomon's splendor
4:20–34

Solomon builds the Lord's temple
5:1–8:66

Solomon's fame and reputation
9:1–10:29

Solomon's sin and death
11:1–43

The Divided Kingdoms of Judah and Israel
1KG 12–22

.
.
.

Judah's King Rehoboam
12:1–24

Israel's King Jeroboam
12:25–14:20

Judah's King Rehoboam (continued)
14:21–31

Judah's Abijam and Asa
15:1–24

Israel's Nadab and Baasha
15:25–16:7

Israel's Elah, Zimri, Tibni, and Omri
16:8–28

Israel's King Ahab and the prophet Elijah
16:29–22:40

Judah's King Jehoshaphat
22:41–50

Israel's King Ahaziah
22:51–53

King David's Last Days

DAY

.

1

✦

. . .

David, Solomon

♀

. . . .

The united kingdom of Israel

1 Kings 1

DAVID'S LAST DAYS

[1] Now King David was old and advanced in age. Although they covered him with bedclothes, he could not get warm. [2] So his servants said to him: "Let us search for a young virgin for my lord the king. She is to attend the king and be his caregiver. She is to lie by your side so that my lord the king will get warm." [3] They searched for a beautiful girl throughout the territory of Israel; they found Abishag the Shunammite and brought her to the king. [4] The girl was of unsurpassed beauty, and she became the king's caregiver. She attended to him, but he was not intimate with her.

ADONIJAH'S BID FOR POWER

[5] Adonijah son of Haggith kept exalting himself, saying, "I will be king!" He prepared chariots, cavalry, and fifty men to run ahead of him. [6] But his father had never once infuriated him by asking, "Why did you do that?" In addition, he was quite handsome and was born after Absalom. [7] He conspired with Joab son of Zeruiah and with the priest Abiathar. They supported Adonijah, [8] but the priest Zadok, Benaiah son of Jehoiada, the prophet Nathan, Shimei, Rei, and David's royal guard did not side with Adonijah.

[9] Adonijah sacrificed sheep, goats, cattle, and fattened cattle near the stone of Zoheleth, which is next to En-rogel. He invited all his royal brothers and all the men of Judah, the servants of the king, [10] but he did not invite the prophet Nathan, Benaiah, the royal guard, or his brother Solomon.

NATHAN'S AND BATHSHEBA'S APPEALS

[11] Then Nathan said to Bathsheba, Solomon's mother, "Have you not heard that Adonijah son of Haggith has become king and our lord David does not know it? [12] Now please come and let me advise you. Save your life and the life of your son Solomon. [13] Go, approach King David and say to him, 'My lord the king, did you not swear to your servant: Your son Solomon is to become king after me, and he is the one who is to sit on my throne? So why has Adonijah become king?' [14] At that moment, while you are still there speaking with the king, I'll come in after you and confirm your words."

[15] So Bathsheba went to the king in his bedroom. Since the king was very old, Abishag the Shunammite was attending to him. [16] Bathsheba knelt low and paid homage to the king, and he asked, "What do you want?"

[17] She replied, "My lord, you swore to your servant by the LORD your God, 'Your son Solomon is to become king after me, and he is the one who is to

sit on my throne.' ¹⁸ Now look, Adonijah has become king. And, my lord the king, you didn't know it. ¹⁹ He has lavishly sacrificed oxen, fattened cattle, and sheep. He invited all the king's sons, the priest Abiathar, and Joab the commander of the army, but he did not invite your servant Solomon. ²⁰ Now, my lord the king, the eyes of all Israel are on you to tell them who will sit on the throne of my lord the king after him. ²¹ Otherwise, when my lord the king rests with his fathers, I and my son Solomon will be regarded as criminals."

²² At that moment, while she was still speaking with the king, the prophet Nathan arrived, ²³ and it was announced to the king, "The prophet Nathan is here." He came into the king's presence and paid homage to him with his face to the ground.

²⁴ "My lord the king," Nathan said, "did you say, 'Adonijah is to become king after me, and he is the one who is to sit on my throne'? ²⁵ For today he went down and lavishly sacrificed oxen, fattened cattle, and sheep. He invited all the sons of the king, the commanders of the army, and the priest Abiathar. And look! They're eating and drinking in his presence, and they're saying, 'Long live King Adonijah!' ²⁶ But he did not invite me—me, your servant—or the priest Zadok or Benaiah son of Jehoiada or your servant Solomon. ²⁷ I'm certain my lord the king would not have let this happen without letting your servant know who will sit on my lord the king's throne after him."

SOLOMON CONFIRMED KING

²⁸ King David responded by saying, "Call in Bathsheba for me." So she came into the king's presence and stood before him. ²⁹ The king swore an oath and said, "As the LORD lives, who has redeemed my life from every difficulty, ³⁰ just as I swore to you by the LORD God of Israel: Your son Solomon is to become king after me, and he is the one who is to sit on my throne in my place, that is exactly what I will do this very day."

³¹ Bathsheba knelt low with her face to the ground, paying homage to the king, and said, "May my lord King David live forever!"

³² King David then said, "Call in the priest Zadok, the prophet Nathan, and Benaiah son of Jehoiada for me." So they came into the king's presence. ³³ The king said to them, "Take my servants with you, have my son Solomon ride on my own mule, and take him down to Gihon. ³⁴ There, the priest Zadok and the prophet Nathan are to anoint him as king over Israel. You are to blow the ram's horn and say, 'Long live King Solomon!' ³⁵ You are to come up after him, and he is to come in and sit on my throne. He is the one who is to become king in my place; he is the one I have commanded to be ruler over Israel and Judah."

³⁶ "Amen," Benaiah son of Jehoiada replied to the king. "May the LORD, the God of my lord the king, so affirm it. ³⁷ Just as the LORD was with my lord the king, so may he be with Solomon and make his throne greater than the throne of my lord King David."

³⁸ Then the priest Zadok, the prophet Nathan, Benaiah son of Jehoiada, the Cherethites, and the Pelethites went down, had Solomon ride on King David's mule, and took him to Gihon. ³⁹ The priest Zadok took the horn of oil from the tabernacle and anointed Solomon. Then they blew the ram's horn, and all the people proclaimed, "Long live King Solomon!" ⁴⁰ All the people went up after him, playing flutes and rejoicing with such a great joy that the earth split open from the sound.

ADONIJAH HEARS OF SOLOMON'S CORONATION

⁴¹ Adonijah and all the invited guests who were with him heard the noise as they finished eating. Joab heard the sound of the ram's horn and said, "Why is the town in such an uproar?" ⁴² He was still speaking when Jonathan son of Abiathar the priest, suddenly arrived. Adonijah said, "Come in, for you are an important man, and you must be bringing good news."

⁴³ "Unfortunately not," Jonathan answered him. "Our lord King David has made Solomon king. ⁴⁴ And with Solomon, the king has sent the priest Zadok, the prophet Nathan, Benaiah son of Jehoiada, the Cherethites, and the Pelethites,

and they have had him ride on the king's mule. ⁴⁵ The priest Zadok and the prophet Nathan have anointed him king in Gihon. They have gone up from there rejoicing. The town has been in an uproar; that's the noise you heard. ⁴⁶ Solomon has even taken his seat on the royal throne.

⁴⁷ "The king's servants have also gone to congratulate our lord King David, saying, 'May your God make the name of Solomon more well known than your name, and may he make his throne greater than your throne.' Then the king bowed in worship on his bed. ⁴⁸ And the king went on to say this: 'Blessed be the LORD God of Israel! Today he has provided one to sit on my throne, and I am a witness.'"

⁴⁹ Then all of Adonijah's guests got up trembling and went their separate ways. ⁵⁰ Adonijah was afraid of Solomon, so he got up and went to take hold of the horns of the altar.

⁵¹ It was reported to Solomon: "Look, Adonijah fears King Solomon, and he has taken hold of the horns of the altar, saying, 'Let King Solomon first swear to me that he will not kill his servant with the sword.'"

⁵² Then Solomon said, "If he is a man of character, not a single hair of his will fall to the ground, but if evil is found in him, he dies." ⁵³ So King Solomon sent for him, and they took him down from the altar. He came and paid homage to King Solomon, and Solomon said to him, "Go to your home."

1 Kings 2

DAVID'S DYING INSTRUCTIONS TO SOLOMON

¹ As the time approached for David to die, he ordered his son Solomon, ² "As for me, I am going the way of all of the earth. Be strong and be a man, ³ and keep your obligation to the LORD your God to walk in his ways and to keep his statutes, commands, ordinances, and decrees. This is written in the law of Moses, so that you will have success in everything you do and wherever you turn, ⁴ and so that the LORD will fulfill his promise that he made to me: 'If your sons guard their way to walk faithfully before me with all their heart and all their soul, you will never fail to have a man on the throne of Israel.'

⁵ "You also know what Joab son of Zeruiah did to me and what he did to the two commanders of Israel's army, Abner son of Ner and Amasa son of Jether. He murdered them in a time of peace to avenge blood shed in war. He spilled that blood on his own waistband and on the sandals of his feet. ⁶ Act according to your wisdom, and do not let his gray head descend to Sheol in peace.

⁷ "Show kindness to the sons of Barzillai the Gileadite and let them be among those who eat at your table because they supported me when I fled from your brother Absalom.

References to the Davidic covenant in the daily readings are marked in gold (see p. 19).

8 "Keep an eye on Shimei son of Gera, the Benjaminite from Bahurim who is with you. He uttered malicious curses against me the day I went to Mahanaim. But he came down to meet me at the Jordan River, and I swore to him by the LORD: 'I will never kill you with the sword.' 9 So don't let him go unpunished, for you are a wise man. You know how to deal with him to bring his gray head down to Sheol with blood."

10 Then David rested with his fathers and was buried in the city of David. 11 The length of time David reigned over Israel was forty years: he reigned seven years in Hebron and thirty-three years in Jerusalem. 12 Solomon sat on the throne of his father David, and his kingship was firmly established.

ADONIJAH'S FOOLISH REQUEST

13 Now Adonijah son of Haggith came to Bathsheba, Solomon's mother. She asked, "Do you come peacefully?"

"Peacefully," he replied, 14 and then asked, "May I talk with you?"

"Go ahead," she answered.

15 "You know the kingship was mine," he said. "All Israel expected me to be king, but then the kingship was turned over to my brother, for the LORD gave it to him. 16 So now I have just one request of you; don't turn me down."

She said to him, "Go on."

17 He replied, "Please speak to King Solomon since he won't turn you down. Let him give me Abishag the Shunammite as a wife."

18 "Very well," Bathsheba replied. "I will speak to the king for you."

19 So Bathsheba went to King Solomon to speak to him about Adonijah. The king stood up to greet her, bowed to her, sat down on his throne, and had a throne placed for the king's mother. So she sat down at his right hand.

20 Then she said, "I have just one small request of you. Don't turn me down."

"Go ahead and ask, mother," the king replied, "for I won't turn you down."

21 So she said, "Let Abishag the Shunammite be given to your brother Adonijah as a wife."

22 King Solomon answered his mother, "Why are you requesting Abishag the Shunammite for Adonijah? Since he is my elder brother, you might as well ask the kingship for him, for the priest Abiathar, and for Joab son of Zeruiah." 23 Then King Solomon took an oath by the LORD: "May God punish me and do so severely if Adonijah has not made this request at the cost of his life. 24 And now, as the LORD lives— the one who established me, seated me on the throne of my father David, and made me a dynasty as he promised— I swear Adonijah will be put to death today!" 25 Then King Solomon dispatched Benaiah son of Jehoiada, who struck down Adonijah, and he died.

ABIATHAR'S BANISHMENT

26 The king said to the priest Abiathar, "Go to your fields in Anathoth. Even though you deserve to die, I will not put you to death today, since you carried the ark of the Lord GOD in the presence of my father David and you suffered through all that my father suffered." 27 So Solomon banished Abiathar from being the LORD's priest, and it fulfilled the LORD's prophecy he had spoken at Shiloh against Eli's family.

JOAB'S EXECUTION

28 The news reached Joab. Since he had supported Adonijah but not Absalom, Joab fled to the LORD's tabernacle and took hold of the horns of the altar.

29 It was reported to King Solomon: "Joab has fled to the LORD's tabernacle and is now beside the altar." Then Solomon sent Benaiah son of Jehoiada and told him, "Go and strike him down!"

30 So Benaiah went to the tabernacle and said to Joab, "This is what the king says: 'Come out!'"

But Joab said, "No, for I will die here."

So Benaiah took a message back to the king, "This is what Joab said, and this is how he answered me."

[31] The king said to him, "Do just as he says. Strike him down and bury him in order to remove from me and from my father's family the blood that Joab shed without just cause. [32] The LORD will bring back his own blood on his head because he struck down two men more righteous and better than he, without my father David's knowledge. With his sword, Joab murdered Abner son of Ner, commander of Israel's army, and Amasa son of Jether, commander of Judah's army. [33] The responsibility for their deaths will come back to Joab and to his descendants forever, but for David, his descendants, his dynasty, and his throne, there will be peace from the Lord forever."

[34] Benaiah son of Jehoiada went up, struck down Joab, and put him to death. He was buried at his house in the wilderness. [35] Then the king appointed Benaiah son of Jehoiada in Joab's place over the army, and he appointed the priest Zadok in Abiathar's place.

SHIMEI'S BANISHMENT AND EXECUTION

[36] Then the king summoned Shimei and said to him, "Build a house for yourself in Jerusalem and live there, but don't leave there and go anywhere else. [37] On the day you do leave and cross the Kidron Valley, know for sure that you will certainly die. Your blood will be on your own head."

[38] Shimei said to the king, "The sentence is fair; your servant will do as my lord the king has spoken." And Shimei lived in Jerusalem for a long time.

[39] But then, at the end of three years, two of Shimei's slaves ran away to Achish son of Maacah, king of Gath. Shimei was informed, "Look, your slaves are in Gath." [40] So Shimei saddled his donkey and set out to Achish at Gath to search for his slaves. He went and brought them back from Gath.

[41] It was reported to Solomon that Shimei had gone from Jerusalem to Gath and had returned. [42] So the king summoned Shimei and said to him, "Didn't I make you swear by the LORD and warn you, saying, 'On the day you leave and go anywhere else, know for sure that you will certainly die'? And you said to me, 'The sentence is fair; I will obey.' [43] So why have you not kept the LORD's oath and the command that I gave you?" [44] The king also said, "You yourself know all the evil that you did to my father David. Therefore, the LORD has brought back your evil on your head, [45] but King Solomon will be blessed, and David's throne will remain established before the Lord forever."

[46] Then the king commanded Benaiah son of Jehoiada, and he went out and struck Shimei down, and he died. So the kingdom was established in Solomon's hand.

2 Samuel 7:12–13

[12] "When your time comes and you rest with your fathers, I will raise up after you your descendant, who will come from your body, and I will establish his kingdom. [13] He is the one who will build a house for my name, and I will establish the throne of his kingdom forever."

NOTES

Now, my lord the king, the eyes of all Israel are on you to tell them who will sit on the throne of my lord the king after him.

1 KINGS 1:20

The Lord Appears to Solomon

1 Kings 3

THE LORD APPEARS TO SOLOMON

¹ Solomon made an alliance with **Pharaoh** king of Egypt by marrying Pharaoh's daughter. Solomon brought her to the city of David until he finished building his palace, the Lord's temple, and the wall surrounding Jerusalem. ² However, the people were sacrificing on the high places, because until that time a temple for the Lord's name had not been built. ³ Solomon loved the Lord by walking in the statutes of his father David, but he also sacrificed and burned incense on the high places.

⁴ The king went to Gibeon to sacrifice there because it was the most famous high place. He offered a thousand burnt offerings on that altar. ⁵ At Gibeon the Lord appeared to Solomon in a dream at night. God said, "Ask. What should I give you?"

⁶ And Solomon replied, "You have shown great and faithful love to your servant, my father David, because he walked before you in faithfulness, righteousness, and integrity. You have continued this great and faithful love for him by giving him a son to sit on his throne, as it is today.

⁷ "Lord my God, you have now made your servant king in my father David's place. Yet I am just a youth with no experience in leadership. ⁸ Your servant is among your people you have chosen, a people too many to be numbered or counted. ⁹ So give your servant a receptive heart to judge your people and to discern between good and evil. For who is able to judge this great people of yours?"

People and deities marked in **bold** are included in the "Neighbors of Israel and Judah" extra on pages 64–67.

¹⁰ Now it pleased the Lord that Solomon had requested this. ¹¹ So God said to him, "Because you have requested this and did not ask for long life or riches for yourself, or the death of your enemies, but you asked discernment for yourself to administer justice, ¹² I will therefore do what you have asked. I will give you a wise and understanding heart, so that there has never been anyone like you before and never will be again. ¹³ In addition, I will give you what you did not ask for: both riches and honor, so that no king will be your equal during your entire life. ¹⁴ If you walk in my ways and keep my statutes and commands just as your father David did, I will give you a long life."

¹⁵ Then Solomon woke up and realized it had been a dream. He went to Jerusalem, stood before the ark of the Lord's covenant, and offered burnt offerings and fellowship offerings. Then he held a feast for all his servants.

SOLOMON'S WISDOM

¹⁶ Then two women who were prostitutes came to the king and stood before him. ¹⁷ One woman said, "Please, my lord, this woman and I live in the same house, and I had a baby while she was in the house. ¹⁸ On the third day after I gave birth, she also had a baby and we were alone. No one else was with us in the house; just the two of us were there. ¹⁹ During the night this woman's son died because she lay on him. ²⁰ She got up in the middle of the night and took my son from my side while your servant was asleep. She laid him in her arms, and she put her dead son in my arms. ²¹ When I got up in the morning to nurse my son, I discovered he was dead. That morning, when I looked closely at him I realized that he was not the son I gave birth to."

²² "No," the other woman said. "My son is the living one; your son is the dead one."

The first woman said, "No, your son is the dead one; my son is the living one." So they argued before the king.

²³ The king replied, "This woman says, 'This is my son who is alive, and your son is dead,' but that woman says, 'No, your son is dead, and my son is alive.'" ²⁴ The king continued, "Bring me a sword." So they brought the sword to the king.

²⁵ And the king said, "Cut the living boy in two and give half to one and half to the other."

²⁶ The woman whose son was alive spoke to the king because she felt great compassion for her son. "My lord, give her the living baby," she said, "but please don't have him killed!"

But the other one said, "He will not be mine or yours. Cut him in two!"

²⁷ The king responded, "Give the living baby to the first woman, and don't kill him. She is his mother." ²⁸ All Israel heard about the judgment the king had given, and they stood in awe of the king because they saw that God's wisdom was in him to carry out justice.

1 Kings 4

SOLOMON'S OFFICIALS

¹ King Solomon reigned over all Israel, ² and these were his officials:

Azariah son of Zadok, priest;
³ Elihoreph and Ahijah the sons of Shisha, secretaries;
Jehoshaphat son of Ahilud, court historian;
⁴ Benaiah son of Jehoiada, in charge of the army;
Zadok and Abiathar, priests;
⁵ Azariah son of Nathan, in charge of the deputies;
Zabud son of Nathan, a priest and adviser to the king;
⁶ Ahishar, in charge of the palace;
and Adoniram son of Abda, in charge of forced labor.

⁷ Solomon had twelve deputies for all Israel. They provided food for the king and his household; each one made provision for one month out of the year. ⁸ These were their names:

Ben-hur, in the hill country of Ephraim;
⁹ Ben-deker, in Makaz, Shaalbim, Beth-shemesh, and Elon-beth-hanan;
¹⁰ Ben-hesed, in Arubboth (he had Socoh and the whole land of Hepher);
¹¹ Ben-abinadab, in all Naphath-dor (Taphath daughter of Solomon was his wife);

¹² Baana son of Ahilud, in Taanach, Megiddo, and all Beth-shean which is beside Zarethan below Jezreel, from Beth-shean to Abel-meholah, as far as the other side of Jokmeam;

¹³ Ben-geber, in Ramoth-gilead (he had the villages of Jair son of Manasseh, which are in Gilead, and he had the region of Argob, which is in Bashan, sixty great cities with walls and bronze bars);

¹⁴ Ahinadab son of Iddo, in Mahanaim;

¹⁵ Ahimaaz, in Naphtali (he also had married a daughter of Solomon—Basemath);

¹⁶ Baana son of Hushai, in Asher and Bealoth;

¹⁷ Jehoshaphat son of Paruah, in Issachar;

¹⁸ Shimei son of Ela, in Benjamin;

¹⁹ Geber son of Uri, in the land of Gilead, the country of King Sihon of the Amorites and of King Og of Bashan.

There was one deputy in the land of Judah.

SOLOMON'S PROVISIONS

²⁰ Judah and Israel were as numerous as the sand by the sea; they were eating, drinking, and rejoicing. ²¹ Solomon ruled all the kingdoms from the Euphrates River to the land of the Philistines and as far as the border of Egypt. They offered tribute and served Solomon all the days of his life.

²² Solomon's provisions for one day were 150 bushels of fine flour and 300 bushels of meal, ²³ ten fattened cattle, twenty range cattle, and a hundred sheep and goats, besides deer, gazelles, roebucks, and pen-fed poultry, ²⁴ for he had dominion over everything west of the Euphrates from Tiphsah to Gaza and over all the kings west of the Euphrates. He had peace on all his surrounding borders. ²⁵ Throughout Solomon's reign, Judah and Israel lived in safety from Dan to Beer-sheba, each person under his own vine and his own fig tree. ²⁶ Solomon had forty thousand stalls of horses for his chariots, and twelve thousand horsemen. ²⁷ Each of those deputies for a month in turn provided food for King Solomon and for everyone who came to King Solomon's table. They neglected nothing. ²⁸ Each man brought the barley and the straw for the chariot teams and the other horses to the required place according to his assignment.

SOLOMON'S WISDOM AND LITERARY GIFTS

²⁹ God gave Solomon wisdom, very great insight, and understanding as vast as the sand on the seashore. ³⁰ Solomon's wisdom was greater than the wisdom of all the people of the East, greater than all the wisdom of Egypt. ³¹ He was wiser than anyone—wiser than Ethan the Ezrahite, and Heman, Calcol, and Darda, sons of Mahol. His reputation extended to all the surrounding nations.

³² Solomon spoke 3,000 proverbs, and his songs numbered 1,005. ³³ He spoke about trees, from the cedar in Lebanon to the hyssop growing out of the wall. He also spoke about animals, birds, reptiles, and fish.

³⁴ Emissaries of all peoples, sent by every king on earth who had heard of his wisdom, came to listen to Solomon's wisdom.

1 Kings 5:1–12

HIRAM'S BUILDING MATERIALS

¹ **King Hiram** of Tyre sent his emissaries to Solomon when he heard that he had been anointed king in his father's place, for Hiram had always been friends with David.

² Solomon sent this message to Hiram: ³ "You know my father David was not able to build a temple for the name of the LORD his God. This was because of the warfare all around him until the LORD put his enemies under his feet. ⁴ The LORD my God has now given me rest on every side; there is no enemy or crisis. ⁵ So I plan to build a temple for the name of the LORD my God, according to what the LORD promised my father David: 'I will put your son on your throne in your place, and he will build the temple for my name.'

⁶ "Therefore, command that cedars from Lebanon be cut down for me. My servants will be with your servants, and I will pay your servants' wages according to whatever you say, for you know that not a man among us knows how to cut timber like the Sidonians."

[7] When Hiram heard Solomon's words, he rejoiced greatly and said, "Blessed be the Lord today! He has given David a wise son to be over this great people!" [8] Then Hiram sent a reply to Solomon, saying, "I have heard your message; I will do everything you want regarding the cedar and cypress timber. [9] My servants will bring the logs down from Lebanon to the sea, and I will make them into rafts to go by sea to the place you indicate. I will break them apart there, and you can take them away. You then can meet my needs by providing my household with food."

[10] So Hiram provided Solomon with all the cedar and cypress timber he wanted, [11] and Solomon provided Hiram with one hundred thousand bushels of wheat as food for his household and one hundred ten thousand gallons of oil from crushed olives. Solomon did this for Hiram year after year.

[12] The Lord gave Solomon wisdom, as he had promised him. There was peace between Hiram and Solomon, and the two of them made a treaty.

Proverbs 15:33

The fear of the Lord is what wisdom teaches,
and humility comes before honor.

James 1:5

Now if any of you lacks wisdom, he should ask God—who gives to all generously and ungrudgingly—and it will be given to him.

Building the Temple

SOLOMON'S WORKFORCE

[13] Then King Solomon drafted forced laborers from all Israel; the labor force numbered thirty thousand men. [14] He sent ten thousand to Lebanon each month in shifts; one month they were in Lebanon, two months they were at home. Adoniram was in charge of the forced labor. [15] Solomon had seventy thousand porters and eighty thousand stonecutters in the mountains, [16] not including his thirty-three hundred deputies in charge of the work. They supervised the people doing the work. [17] The king commanded them to quarry large, costly stones to lay the foundation of the temple with dressed stones. [18] So Solomon's builders and Hiram's builders, along with the Gebalites, quarried the stone and prepared the timber and stone for the temple's construction.

1 Kings 6

BUILDING THE TEMPLE

[1] Solomon began to build the temple for the LORD in the four hundred eightieth year after the Israelites came out of the land of Egypt, in the fourth year of his reign over Israel, in the month of Ziv, which is the second month. [2] The temple that King Solomon built for the LORD was ninety feet long, thirty feet wide, and forty-five feet high. [3] The portico in front of the temple sanctuary was thirty feet long extending across the temple's width, and fifteen feet deep in front of the temple. [4] He also made windows with beveled frames for the temple.

[5] He then built a chambered structure along the temple wall, encircling the walls of the temple, that is, the sanctuary and the inner sanctuary. And he made side chambers all around. [6] The lowest chamber was 7½ feet wide, the middle was 9 feet wide, and the third was 10½ feet wide. He also provided offset ledges for the temple all around the outside so that nothing would be inserted into the temple walls. [7] The temple's construction used finished stones cut at the quarry so that no hammer, chisel, or any iron tool was heard in the temple while it was being built.

[8] The door for the lowest side chamber was on the right side of the temple. They went up a stairway to the middle chamber, and from the middle to the third. [9] When he finished building the temple, he paneled it with boards and planks of cedar. [10] He built the chambers along the entire temple, joined to the temple with cedar beams; each story was 7½ feet high.

¹¹ The word of the LORD came to Solomon: ¹² "As for this temple you are building—if you walk in my statutes, observe my ordinances, and keep all my commands by walking in them, I will fulfill my promise to you, which I made to your father David. ¹³ I will dwell among the Israelites and not abandon my people Israel."

¹⁴ When Solomon finished building the temple, ¹⁵ he paneled the interior temple walls with cedar boards; from the temple floor to the surface of the ceiling he overlaid the interior with wood. He also overlaid the floor with cypress boards. ¹⁶ Then he lined thirty feet of the rear of the temple with cedar boards from the floor to the surface of the ceiling, and he built the interior as an inner sanctuary, the most holy place. ¹⁷ The temple, that is, the sanctuary in front of the most holy place, was sixty feet long. ¹⁸ The cedar paneling inside the temple was carved with ornamental gourds and flower blossoms. Everything was cedar; not a stone could be seen.

¹⁹ He prepared the inner sanctuary inside the temple to put the ark of the LORD's covenant there. ²⁰ The interior of the sanctuary was thirty feet long, thirty feet wide, and thirty feet high; he overlaid it with pure gold. He also overlaid the cedar altar. ²¹ Next, Solomon overlaid the interior of the temple with pure gold, and he hung gold chains across the front of the inner sanctuary and overlaid it with gold. ²² So he added the gold overlay to the entire temple until everything was completely finished, including the entire altar that belongs to the inner sanctuary.

²³ In the inner sanctuary he made two cherubim 15 feet high out of olive wood. ²⁴ One wing of the first cherub was 7½ feet long, and the other wing was 7½ feet long. The wingspan was 15 feet from tip to tip. ²⁵ The second cherub also was 15 feet; both cherubim had the same size and shape. ²⁶ The first cherub's height was 15 feet and so was the second cherub's. ²⁷ Then he put the cherubim inside the inner temple. Since their wings were spread out, the first one's wing touched one wall while the second cherub's wing touched the other wall, and in the middle of the temple their wings were touching wing to wing. ²⁸ He also overlaid the cherubim with gold.

²⁹ He carved all the surrounding temple walls with carved engravings—cherubim, palm trees, and flower blossoms—in the inner and outer sanctuaries. ³⁰ He overlaid the temple floor with gold in both the inner and the outer sanctuaries.

³¹ For the entrance of the inner sanctuary, he made olive wood doors. The pillars of the doorposts were five-sided. ³² The two doors were made of olive wood. He carved cherubim, palm trees, and flower blossoms on them and overlaid them with gold, hammering gold over the cherubim and palm trees. ³³ In the same way, he made four-sided olive wood doorposts for the sanctuary entrance. ³⁴ The two doors were made of cypress wood; the first door had two folding sides, and the second door had two folding panels. ³⁵ He carved cherubim, palm trees, and flower blossoms on them and overlaid them with gold applied evenly over the carving. ³⁶ He built the inner courtyard with three rows of dressed stone and a row of trimmed cedar beams.

³⁷ The foundation of the LORD's temple was laid in Solomon's fourth year in the month of Ziv. ³⁸ In his eleventh year in the month of Bul, which is the eighth month, the temple was completed in every detail and according to every specification. So he built it in seven years.

1 Kings 7

SOLOMON'S PALACE COMPLEX

¹ Solomon completed his entire palace complex after thirteen years of construction. ² He built the House of the Forest of Lebanon. It was one hundred fifty feet long, seventy-five feet wide, and forty-five feet high on four rows of cedar pillars, with cedar beams on top of the pillars. ³ It was paneled above with cedar at the top of the chambers that rested on forty-five pillars, fifteen per row. ⁴ There were three rows of window frames, facing each other in three tiers. ⁵ All the doors and doorposts had rectangular frames, the openings facing each other in three tiers. ⁶ He made the hall of pillars seventy-five feet long and forty-five feet wide. A portico was in front of the pillars, and a canopy with pillars was in front of them. ⁷ He made the Hall of the Throne where he would judge—the Hall of Judgment. It was paneled with cedar from the floor to the rafters. ⁸ Solomon's own palace where he would live, in the other courtyard behind the hall, was of similar construction. And he made a house like this hall for Pharaoh's daughter, his wife.

⁹ All of these buildings were of costly stones, cut to size and sawed with saws on the inner and outer surfaces, from foundation to coping and from the outside to the great courtyard. ¹⁰ The foundation was made of large, costly stones twelve and fifteen feet long. ¹¹ Above were also costly stones, cut to size, as well as cedar wood. ¹² Around the great courtyard, as well as the inner courtyard of the Lord's temple and the portico of the temple, were three rows of dressed stone and a row of trimmed cedar beams.

¹³ King Solomon had **Hiram** brought from Tyre. ¹⁴ He was a widow's son from the tribe of Naphtali, and his father was a man of Tyre, a bronze craftsman. Hiram had great skill, understanding, and knowledge to do every kind of bronze work. So he came to King Solomon and carried out all his work.

THE BRONZE PILLARS

¹⁵ He cast two bronze pillars, each 27 feet high and 18 feet in circumference. ¹⁶ He also made two capitals of cast bronze to set on top of the pillars; 7½ feet was the height of the first capital, and 7½ feet was also the height of the second capital. ¹⁷ The capitals on top of the pillars had gratings of latticework, wreaths made of chainwork—seven for the first capital and seven for the second.

¹⁸ He made the pillars with two encircling rows of pomegranates on the one grating to cover the capital on top; he did the same for the second capital. ¹⁹ And the capitals on top of the pillars in the portico were shaped like lilies, six feet high. ²⁰ The capitals on the two pillars were also immediately above the rounded surface next to the grating, and two hundred pomegranates were in rows encircling each capital. ²¹ He set up the pillars at the portico of the sanctuary: he set up the right pillar and named it Jachin; then he set up the left pillar and named it Boaz. ²² The tops of the pillars were shaped like lilies. Then the work of the pillars was completed.

THE BASIN

²³ He made the cast metal basin, 15 feet from brim to brim, perfectly round. It was 7½ feet high and 45 feet in circumference. ²⁴ Ornamental gourds encircled it below the brim, ten every half yard, completely encircling the basin. The gourds were cast in two rows when the basin was cast. ²⁵ It stood on twelve oxen, three facing north, three facing west, three facing south, and three facing east. The basin was on top of them and all their hindquarters were toward the center. ²⁶ The basin was three inches thick, and its rim was fashioned like the brim of a cup or of a lily blossom. It held eleven thousand gallons.

THE BRONZE WATER CARTS

²⁷ Then he made ten bronze water carts. Each water cart was 6 feet long, 6 feet wide, and 4½ feet high. ²⁸ This was the design of the carts: They had frames; the frames were between the cross-pieces, ²⁹ and on the frames between the cross-pieces were lions, oxen, and cherubim. On the cross-pieces there was a pedestal

above, and below the lions and oxen were wreaths of hanging work. ³⁰ Each cart had four bronze wheels with bronze axles. Underneath the four corners of the basin were cast supports, each next to a wreath. ³¹ And the water cart's opening inside the crown on top was eighteen inches wide. The opening was round, made as a pedestal twenty-seven inches wide. On it were carvings, but their frames were square, not round. ³² There were four wheels under the frames, and the wheel axles were part of the water cart; each wheel was twenty-seven inches tall. ³³ The wheels' design was similar to that of chariot wheels: their axles, rims, spokes, and hubs were all of cast metal. ³⁴ Four supports were at the four corners of each water cart; each support was one piece with the water cart. ³⁵ At the top of the cart was a band nine inches high encircling it; also, at the top of the cart, its braces and its frames were one piece with it. ³⁶ He engraved cherubim, lions, and palm trees on the plates of its braces and on its frames, wherever each had space, with encircling wreaths. ³⁷ In this way he made the ten water carts using the same casting, dimensions, and shape for all of them.

BRONZE BASINS AND OTHER UTENSILS

³⁸ Then he made ten bronze basins—each basin held 220 gallons and each was six feet wide—one basin for each of the ten water carts. ³⁹ He set five water carts on the right side of the temple and five on the left side. He put the basin near the right side of the temple toward the southeast. ⁴⁰ Then Hiram made the basins, the shovels, and the sprinkling basins.

COMPLETION OF THE BRONZE WORKS

So Hiram finished all the work that he was doing for King Solomon on the LORD's temple: ⁴¹ two pillars; bowls for the capitals that were on top of the two pillars; the two gratings for covering both bowls of the capitals that were on top of the pillars; ⁴² the four hundred pomegranates for the two gratings (two rows of pomegranates for each grating covering both capitals' bowls on top of the pillars); ⁴³ the ten water carts; the ten basins on the water carts; ⁴⁴ the basin; the twelve oxen underneath the basin; ⁴⁵ and the pots, shovels, and sprinkling basins. All the utensils that Hiram made for King Solomon at the LORD's temple were made of burnished bronze. ⁴⁶ The king had them cast in clay molds in the Jordan Valley between Succoth and Zarethan. ⁴⁷ Solomon left all the utensils unweighed because there were so many; the weight of the bronze was not determined.

COMPLETION OF THE GOLD FURNISHINGS

⁴⁸ Solomon also made all the equipment in the LORD's temple: the gold altar; the gold table that the Bread of the Presence was placed on; ⁴⁹ the pure gold lampstands in front of the inner sanctuary, five on the right and five on the left; the gold flowers, lamps, and tongs; ⁵⁰ the pure gold ceremonial bowls, wick trimmers, sprinkling basins, ladles, and firepans; and the gold hinges for the doors of the inner temple (that is, the most holy place) and for the doors of the temple sanctuary.

⁵¹ So all the work King Solomon did in the LORD's temple was completed. Then Solomon brought in the consecrated things of his father David—the silver, the gold, and the utensils—and put them in the treasuries of the LORD's temple.

Leviticus 26:11–13

¹¹ "I will place my residence among you, and I will not reject you. ¹² I will walk among you and be your God, and you will be my people. ¹³ I am the LORD your God, who brought you out of the land of Egypt, so that you would no longer be their slaves. I broke the bars of your yoke and enabled you to live in freedom."

Ephesians 2:19–22

¹⁹ So then you are no longer foreigners and strangers, but fellow citizens with the saints, and members of God's household, ²⁰ built on the foundation of the apostles and prophets, with Christ Jesus himself as the cornerstone. ²¹ In him the whole building, being put together, grows into a holy temple in the Lord. ²² In him you are also being built together for God's dwelling in the Spirit.

NOTES

Solomon's Temple

Solomon started building the temple on Mount Moriah in Jerusalem in 967 BC (1Kg 6:1; 2Ch 3:1–2). The temple was completed seven years later in 960 BC (1Kg 6:38). The temple structure, which stood in the middle of the court, was 90 feet long, 30 feet wide, and 45 feet high.

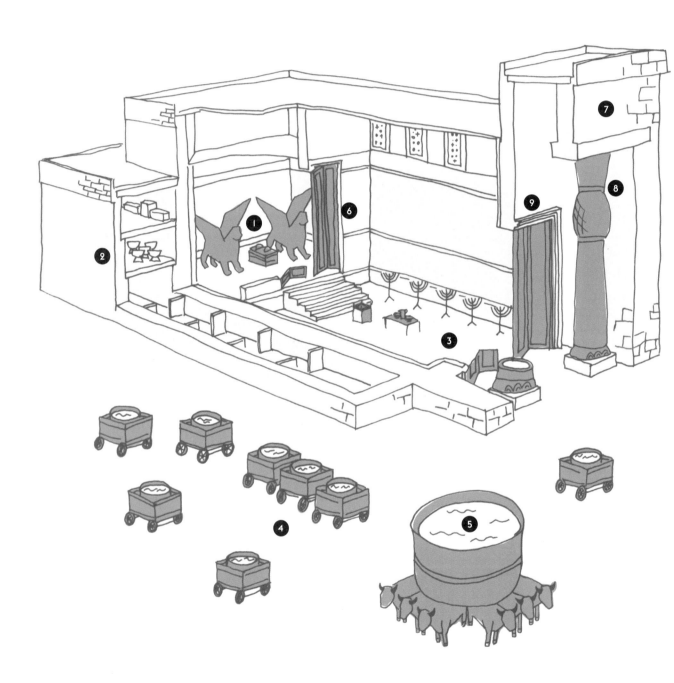

1

THE MOST HOLY PLACE

1KG 6:15–29; 8:1–11; 2CH 3:8–14; 5:7–10

Contained two large golden cherubim, which stood on either side of the ark. Each cherub was 15 feet tall with a 15-foot wingspan.

2

THREE-LEVEL STRUCTURE

1KG 6:5–6, 8, 10

Built around the temple walls. The lower chamber was 7½ feet wide, the middle chamber was 9 feet wide, and the upper chamber was 10½ feet wide.

3

THE HOLY PLACE

1KG 6:15, 17–18; 7:48–49; 2CH 3:5–7; 2CH 4:7

Contained the golden altar of incense, the golden table for the bread of the presence, and ten golden lampstands. It measured 60 feet long by 30 feet wide.

4

TEN LARGE BASINS

1KG 7:27–38; 2CH 4:6

On stands with bronze wheels. The basins contained water for cleaning animal parts used for burnt offerings.

5

METAL BASIN CALLED "THE SEA"

1KG 7:23–26; 2CH 4:2–5

Supported by twelve bronze oxen arranged in sets of three. It measured 7½ feet high, 15 feet in diameter, and held 11,000 gallons of water for the priest's ceremonial purification.

6

GOLD-COVERED WOODEN DOORS

1KG 6:31–32

Separated the most holy place from the holy place.

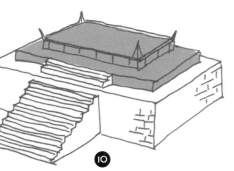

7

PORTICO

1KG 6:3; 2CH 3:4

Thirty feet wide by 15 feet deep.

8

HOLLOW BRONZE PILLARS

1KG 7:21; 2CH 3:17

The right pillar was called Boaz, "In Him Is Strength." The left pillar was called Jachin, "He Will Establish."

9

GOLD-COVERED WOODEN DOORS

1KG 6:33–35

Separated the holy place from the portico.

10

BRONZE ALTAR

2CH 4:1

For burnt offerings. It measured 15 feet high by 30 feet long and wide.

Solomon's Prayer

Solomon

The united kingdom of Israel

SOLOMON'S DEDICATION OF THE TEMPLE

¹ At that time Solomon assembled the elders of Israel, all the tribal heads and the ancestral leaders of the Israelites before him at Jerusalem in order to bring the ark of the Lord's covenant from the city of David, that is Zion. ² So all the men of Israel were assembled in the presence of King Solomon in the month of Ethanim, which is the seventh month, at the festival.

³ All the elders of Israel came, and the priests picked up the ark. ⁴ The priests and the Levites brought the ark of the Lord, the tent of meeting, and the holy utensils that were in the tent. ⁵ King Solomon and the entire congregation of Israel, who had gathered around him and were with him in front of the ark, were sacrificing sheep, goats, and cattle that could not be counted or numbered, because there were so many. ⁶ The priests brought the ark of the Lord's covenant to its place, into the inner sanctuary of the temple, to the most holy place beneath the wings of the cherubim. ⁷ For the cherubim were spreading their wings over the place of the ark, so that the cherubim covered the ark and its poles from above. ⁸ The poles were so long that their ends were seen from the holy place in front of the inner sanctuary, but they were not seen from outside the sanctuary; they are still there today. ⁹ Nothing was in the ark except the two stone tablets that Moses had put there at Horeb, where the Lord made a covenant with the Israelites when they came out of the land of Egypt.

¹⁰ When the priests came out of the holy place, the cloud filled the Lord's temple, ¹¹ and because of the cloud, the priests were not able to continue ministering, for the glory of the Lord filled the temple.

¹² Then Solomon said:

> The Lord said that he would dwell in total darkness.
> ¹³ I have indeed built an exalted temple for you,
> a place for your dwelling forever.

¹⁴ The king turned around and blessed the entire congregation of Israel while they were standing. ¹⁵ He said:

> Blessed be the Lord God of Israel!
> He spoke directly to my father David,
> and he has fulfilled the promise by his power.
> He said,
> ¹⁶ "Since the day I brought my people Israel out of Egypt,
> I have not chosen a city to build a temple in

among any of the tribes of Israel,

so that my name would be there.

But I have chosen David to rule my people Israel."

¹⁷ My father David had his heart set

on building a temple for the name of the LORD,

　　the God of Israel.

¹⁸ But the LORD said to my father David,

"Since your heart was set on building a temple

　　for my name,

you have done well to have this desire.

¹⁹ Yet you are not the one to build it;

instead, your son, your own offspring,

will build it for my name."

²⁰ The LORD has fulfilled what he promised.

I have taken the place of my father David,

and I sit on the throne of Israel, as the LORD promised.

I have built the temple for the name of the LORD,

　　the God of Israel.

²¹ I have provided a place there for the ark,

where the LORD's covenant is

that he made with our ancestors

when he brought them out of the land of Egypt.

SOLOMON'S PRAYER

²² Then Solomon stood before the altar of the LORD in front of the entire congregation of Israel and spread out his hands toward heaven. ²³ He said:

LORD God of Israel,

there is no God like you

in heaven above or on earth below,

who keeps the gracious covenant

with your servants who walk before you

with all their heart.

²⁴ You have kept what you promised

to your servant, my father David.

You spoke directly to him

and you fulfilled your promise by your power

as it is today.

²⁵ Therefore, LORD God of Israel,

keep what you promised

to your servant, my father David:

You will never fail to have a man

to sit before me on the throne of Israel,

if only your sons take care to walk before me

as you have walked before me.

²⁶ Now LORD God of Israel,

please confirm what you promised

to your servant, my father David.

²⁷ But will God indeed live on earth?

Even heaven, the highest heaven, cannot contain you,

much less this temple I have built.

²⁸ Listen to your servant's prayer and his petition,

LORD my God,

so that you may hear the cry and the prayer

that your servant prays before you today,

²⁹ so that your eyes may watch over this temple night

　　and day,

toward the place where you said,

"My name will be there,"

and so that you may hear the prayer

that your servant prays toward this place.

³⁰ Hear the petition of your servant

and your people Israel,

which they pray toward this place.

May you hear in your dwelling place in heaven.

May you hear and forgive.

³¹ When a man sins against his neighbor

and is forced to take an oath,

and he comes to take an oath

before your altar in this temple,

³² may you hear in heaven and act.

May you judge your servants,

condemning the wicked man by bringing

what he has done on his own head

and providing justice for the righteous

by rewarding him according to his righteousness.

³³ When your people Israel are defeated before an enemy,

because they have sinned against you,

and they return to you and praise your name,

and they pray and plead with you

for mercy in this temple,

³⁴ may you hear in heaven

and forgive the sin of your people Israel.

May you restore them to the land
you gave their ancestors.
[35] When the skies are shut and there is no rain,
because they have sinned against you,
and they pray toward this place
and praise your name,
and they turn from their sins
because you are afflicting them,
[36] may you hear in heaven
and forgive the sin of your servants
and your people Israel,
so that you may teach them the good way
they should walk in.
May you send rain on your land
that you gave your people for an inheritance.
[37] When there is famine in the land,
when there is pestilence,
when there is blight or mildew, locust or grasshopper,
when their enemy besieges them
in the land and its cities,
when there is any plague or illness,
[38] every prayer or petition
that any person or that all your people Israel may have—
they each know their own affliction—
as they spread out their hands toward this temple,
[39] may you hear in heaven, your dwelling place,
and may you forgive, act, and give to everyone
according to all their ways, since you know each heart,
for you alone know every human heart,
[40] so that they may fear you
all the days they live on the land
you gave our ancestors.
[41] Even for the foreigner who is not of your people Israel
but has come from a distant land
because of your name—
[42] for they will hear of your great name,
strong hand, and outstretched arm,
and will come and pray toward this temple—
[43] may you hear in heaven, your dwelling place,
and do according to all the foreigner asks.
Then all peoples of earth will know your name,
to fear you as your people Israel do
and to know that this temple I have built
bears your name.

[44] When your people go out to fight against their enemies,
wherever you send them,
and they pray to the LORD
in the direction of the city you have chosen
and the temple I have built for your name,
[45] may you hear their prayer and petition in heaven
and uphold their cause.
[46] When they sin against you—
for there is no one who does not sin—
and you are angry with them
and hand them over to the enemy,
and their captors deport them to the enemy's country—
whether distant or nearby—
[47] and when they come to their senses
in the land where they were deported
and repent and petition you in their captors' land:
"We have sinned and done wrong;
we have been wicked,"
[48] and when they return to you with all their heart
and all their soul
in the land of their enemies who took them captive,
and when they pray to you in the direction of their land
that you gave their ancestors,
the city you have chosen,
and the temple I have built for your name,
[49] may you hear in heaven, your dwelling place,
their prayer and petition and uphold their cause.
[50] May you forgive your people
who sinned against you
and all their rebellions against you,
and may you grant them compassion
before their captors,
so that they may treat them compassionately.
[51] For they are your people and your inheritance;
you brought them out of Egypt,
out of the middle of an iron furnace.
[52] May your eyes be open to your servant's petition
and to the petition of your people Israel,
listening to them whenever they call to you.
[53] For you, Lord GOD, have set them apart as
your inheritance
from all peoples of the earth,
as you spoke through your servant Moses
when you brought our ancestors out of Egypt.

May all the peoples of the earth know that the Lord is God. There is no other!

SOLOMON'S BLESSING

⁵⁴ When Solomon finished praying this entire prayer and petition to the Lord, he got up from kneeling before the altar of the Lord, with his hands spread out toward heaven, ⁵⁵ and he stood and blessed the whole congregation of Israel with a loud voice: ⁵⁶ "Blessed be the Lord! He has given rest to his people Israel according to all he has said. Not one of all the good promises he made through his servant Moses has failed. ⁵⁷ May the Lord our God be with us as he was with our ancestors. May he not abandon us or leave us ⁵⁸ so that he causes us to be devoted to him, to walk in all his ways, and to keep his commands, statutes, and ordinances, which he commanded our ancestors. ⁵⁹ May my words with which I have made my petition before the Lord be near the Lord our God day and night. May he uphold his servant's cause and the cause of his people Israel, as each day requires. ⁶⁰ May all the peoples of the earth know that the Lord is God. There is no other! ⁶¹ Be wholeheartedly devoted to the Lord our God to walk in his statutes and to keep his commands, as it is today."

⁶² The king and all Israel with him were offering sacrifices in the Lord's presence. ⁶³ Solomon offered a sacrifice of fellowship offerings to the Lord: twenty-two thousand cattle and one hundred twenty thousand sheep and goats. In this manner the king and all the Israelites dedicated the Lord's temple.

⁶⁴ On the same day, the king consecrated the middle of the courtyard that was in front of the Lord's temple because that was where he offered the burnt offering, the grain offering, and the fat of the fellowship offerings since the bronze altar before the Lord was too small to accommodate the burnt offerings, the grain offerings, and the fat of the fellowship offerings.

⁶⁵ Solomon and all Israel with him—a great assembly, from the entrance of Hamath to the Brook of Egypt—observed the festival at that time in the presence of the Lord our God, seven days, and seven more days—fourteen days. ⁶⁶ On the fifteenth day he sent the people away. So they blessed the king and went to their homes rejoicing and with happy hearts for all the goodness that the Lord had done for his servant David and for his people Israel.

1 Kings 9

THE LORD'S RESPONSE

¹ When Solomon finished building the temple of the Lord, the royal palace, and all that Solomon desired to do, ² the Lord appeared to Solomon a second time just as he had appeared to him at Gibeon. ³ The Lord said to him:

I have heard your prayer and petition you have made before me. I have consecrated this temple you have built, to put my name there forever; my eyes and my heart will be there at all times.

⁴ As for you, if you walk before me as your father David walked, with a heart of integrity and in what is right, doing everything I have commanded you, and if you keep my statutes and ordinances, ⁵ I will establish your royal throne over Israel forever, as I promised your father David: You will never fail to have a man on the throne of Israel.

⁶ If you or your sons turn away from following me and do not keep my commands—my statutes that I have set before you—and if you go and serve other gods and bow in worship to them, ⁷ I will cut off Israel from the land I gave them, and I will reject the temple I have sanctified for my name. Israel will become an object of scorn and ridicule among all the peoples. ⁸ Though this temple is now exalted, everyone who passes by will be appalled and will scoff. They will say: Why did the LORD do this to this land and this temple? ⁹ Then they will say: Because they abandoned the LORD their God who brought their ancestors out of the land of Egypt. They held on to other gods and bowed in worship to them and served them. Because of this, the LORD brought all this ruin on them.

KING HIRAM'S TWENTY TOWNS

¹⁰ At the end of twenty years during which Solomon had built the two houses, the LORD's temple and the royal palace— ¹¹ King Hiram of Tyre having supplied him with cedar and cypress logs and gold for his every wish—King Solomon gave Hiram twenty towns in the land of Galilee. ¹² So Hiram went out from Tyre to look over the towns that Solomon had given him, but he was not pleased with them. ¹³ So he said, "What are these towns you've given me, my brother?" So he called them the Land of Cabul, as they are still called today. ¹⁴ Now Hiram had sent the king nine thousand pounds of gold.

SOLOMON'S FORCED LABOR

¹⁵ This is the account of the forced labor that King Solomon had imposed to build the LORD's temple, his own palace, the supporting terraces, the wall of Jerusalem, and Hazor, Megiddo, and Gezer. ¹⁶ Pharaoh king of Egypt had attacked and captured Gezer. He then burned it, killed the Canaanites who lived in the city, and gave it as a dowry to his daughter, Solomon's wife. ¹⁷ Then Solomon rebuilt Gezer, Lower Beth-horon, ¹⁸ Baalath, Tamar in the Wilderness of Judah, ¹⁹ all the storage cities that belonged to Solomon, the chariot cities, the cavalry cities, and whatever Solomon desired to build in Jerusalem, Lebanon, or anywhere else in the land of his dominion.

²⁰ As for all the peoples who remained of the Amorites, Hethites, Perizzites, Hivites, and Jebusites, who were not Israelites— ²¹ their descendants who remained in the land after them, those whom the Israelites were unable to destroy completely—Solomon imposed forced labor on them; it is still this way today. ²² But Solomon did not consign the Israelites to slavery; they were soldiers, his servants, his commanders, his captains, and commanders of his chariots and his cavalry. ²³ These were the deputies who were over Solomon's work: 550 who supervised the people doing the work.

SOLOMON'S OTHER ACTIVITIES

²⁴ Pharaoh's daughter moved from the city of David to the house that Solomon had built for her; he then built the terraces.

²⁵ Three times a year Solomon offered burnt offerings and fellowship offerings on the altar he had built for the LORD, and he burned incense with them in the LORD's presence. So he completed the temple.

²⁶ King Solomon put together a fleet of ships at Ezion-geber, which is near Eloth on the shore of the Red Sea in the land of Edom. ²⁷ With the fleet, Hiram sent his servants, experienced seamen, along with Solomon's servants. ²⁸ They went to Ophir and acquired gold there—sixteen tons—and delivered it to Solomon.

Exodus 25:10–22

THE ARK

¹⁰ "They are to make an ark of acacia wood, forty-five inches long, twenty-seven inches wide, and twenty-seven inches high. ¹¹ Overlay it with pure gold; overlay it both inside and out. Also make a gold molding all around it. ¹² Cast four gold rings for it and place them on its four feet, two rings on one side and two rings on the other side. ¹³ Make poles of acacia wood and overlay them with gold. ¹⁴ Insert the poles

into the rings on the sides of the ark in order to carry the ark with them. [15] The poles are to remain in the rings of the ark; they must not be removed from it. [16] Put the tablets of the testimony that I will give you into the ark. [17] Make a mercy seat of pure gold, forty-five inches long and twenty-seven inches wide. [18] Make two cherubim of gold; make them of hammered work at the two ends of the mercy seat. [19] Make one cherub at one end and one cherub at the other end. At its two ends, make the cherubim of one piece with the mercy seat. [20] The cherubim are to have wings spread out above, covering the mercy seat with their wings, and are to face one another. The faces of the cherubim should be toward the mercy seat. [21] Set the mercy seat on top of the ark and put the tablets of the testimony that I will give you into the ark.

[22] I will meet with you there above the mercy seat, between the two cherubim that are over the ark of the testimony; I will speak with you from there about all that I command you regarding the Israelites."

Solomon's Unfaithfulness to God

DAY

5

Solomon

The united kingdom of Israel

1 Kings 10

THE QUEEN OF SHEBA

¹ The queen of Sheba heard about Solomon's fame connected with the name of the LORD and came to test him with riddles. ² She came to Jerusalem with a very large entourage, with camels bearing spices, gold in great abundance, and precious stones. She came to Solomon and spoke to him about everything that was on her mind. ³ So Solomon answered all her questions; nothing was too difficult for the king to explain to her. ⁴ When the queen of Sheba observed all of Solomon's wisdom, the palace he had built, ⁵ the food at his table, his servants' residence, his attendants' service and their attire, his cupbearers, and the burnt offerings he offered at the LORD's temple, it took her breath away.

⁶ She said to the king, "The report I heard in my own country about your words and about your wisdom is true. ⁷ But I didn't believe the reports until I came and saw with my own eyes. Indeed, I was not even told half. Your wisdom and prosperity far exceed the report I heard. ⁸ How happy are your men. How happy are these servants of yours, who always stand in your presence hearing your wisdom. ⁹ Blessed be the LORD your God! He delighted in you and put you on the throne of Israel, because of the LORD's eternal love for Israel. He has made you king to carry out justice and righteousness."

¹⁰ Then she gave the king four and a half tons of gold, a great quantity of spices, and precious stones. Never again did such a quantity of spices arrive as those the queen of Sheba gave to King Solomon.

¹¹ In addition, Hiram's fleet that carried gold from Ophir brought from Ophir a large quantity of almug wood and precious stones. ¹² The king made the almug wood into steps for the LORD's temple and the king's palace and into lyres and harps for the singers. Never before did such almug wood arrive, and the like has not been seen again.

¹³ King Solomon gave the queen of Sheba her every desire—whatever she asked—besides what he had given her out of his royal bounty. Then she, along with her servants, returned to her own country.

SOLOMON'S WEALTH

¹⁴ The weight of gold that came to Solomon annually was twenty-five tons, ¹⁵ besides what came from merchants, traders' merchandise, and all the Arabian kings and governors of the land.

¹⁶ King Solomon made two hundred large shields of hammered gold; fifteen pounds of gold went into each shield. ¹⁷ He made three hundred

"Yet I will not tear the entire kingdom away from him. I will give one tribe to your son for the sake of my servant David and for the sake of Jerusalem that I chose."

small shields of hammered gold; nearly four pounds of gold went into each shield. The king put them in the House of the Forest of Lebanon.

[18] The king also made a large ivory throne and overlaid it with fine gold. [19] The throne had six steps; there was a rounded top at the back of the throne, armrests on either side of the seat, and two lions standing beside the armrests. [20] Twelve lions were standing there on the six steps, one at each end. Nothing like it had ever been made in any other kingdom.

[21] All of King Solomon's drinking cups were gold, and all the utensils of the House of the Forest of Lebanon were pure gold. There was no silver, since it was considered as nothing in Solomon's time, [22] for the king had ships of Tarshish at sea with Hiram's fleet, and once every three years the ships of Tarshish would arrive bearing gold, silver, ivory, apes, and peacocks.

[23] King Solomon surpassed all the kings of the world in riches and in wisdom. [24] The whole world wanted an audience with Solomon to hear the wisdom that God had put in his heart. [25] Every man would bring his annual tribute: items of silver and gold, clothing, weapons, spices, and horses and mules.

[26] Solomon accumulated 1,400 chariots and 12,000 horsemen and stationed them in the chariot cities and with the king in Jerusalem. [27] The king made silver as common in Jerusalem as stones, and he made cedar as abundant as sycamore in the Judean foothills. [28] Solomon's horses were imported from Egypt and Kue. The king's traders bought them from Kue at the going price. [29] A chariot was imported from Egypt for fifteen pounds of silver, and a horse for nearly four pounds. In the same way, they exported them to all the kings of the Hittites and to the kings of Aram through their agents.

1 Kings 11

SOLOMON'S UNFAITHFULNESS TO GOD

[1] King Solomon loved many foreign women in addition to Pharaoh's daughter: Moabite, Ammonite, Edomite, Sidonian, and Hittite women [2] from the nations about which the LORD had told the Israelites, "You must not intermarry with them, and they must not intermarry with you, because they will turn your heart away to follow their gods." To these women Solomon was deeply attached in love. [3] He had seven hundred wives who were princesses and three hundred who were concubines, and they turned his heart away.

[4] When Solomon was old, his wives turned his heart away to follow other gods. He was not wholeheartedly devoted to the LORD his God, as his father David had been. [5] Solomon followed **Ashtoreth**, the goddess of the Sidonians, and **Milcom**,

the abhorrent idol of the Ammonites. ⁶ Solomon did what was evil in the LORD's sight, and unlike his father David, he did not remain loyal to the LORD.

⁷ At that time, Solomon built a high place for **Chemosh**, the abhorrent idol of Moab, and for Milcom, the abhorrent idol of the Ammonites, on the hill across from Jerusalem. ⁸ He did the same for all his foreign wives, who were burning incense and offering sacrifices to their gods.

⁹ The LORD was angry with Solomon, because his heart had turned away from the LORD, the God of Israel, who had appeared to him twice. ¹⁰ He had commanded him about this, so that he would not follow other gods, but Solomon did not do what the LORD had commanded.

¹¹ Then the LORD said to Solomon, "Since you have done this and did not keep my covenant and my statutes, which I commanded you, I will tear the kingdom away from you and give it to your servant. ¹² However, I will not do it during your lifetime for the sake of your father David; I will tear it out of your son's hand. ¹³ Yet I will not tear the entire kingdom away from him. I will give one tribe to your son for the sake of my servant David and for the sake of Jerusalem that I chose."

SOLOMON'S ENEMIES

¹⁴ So the LORD raised up **Hadad** the Edomite as an enemy against Solomon. He was of the royal family in Edom. ¹⁵ Earlier, when David was in Edom, Joab, the commander of the army, had gone to bury the dead and had struck down every male in Edom. ¹⁶ For Joab and all Israel had remained there six months, until he had killed every male in Edom. ¹⁷ Hadad fled to Egypt, along with some Edomites from his father's servants. At the time Hadad was a small boy. ¹⁸ Hadad and his men set out from Midian and went to Paran. They took men with them from Paran and went to Egypt, to Pharaoh king of Egypt, who gave Hadad a house, ordered that he be given food, and gave him land. ¹⁹ Pharaoh liked Hadad so much that he gave him a wife, the sister of his own wife, **Queen Tahpenes**. ²⁰ Tahpenes's sister gave birth to Hadad's son Genubath. Tahpenes herself weaned him in Pharaoh's palace, and Genubath lived there along with Pharaoh's sons.

²¹ When Hadad heard in Egypt that David rested with his fathers and that Joab, the commander of the army, was dead, Hadad said to Pharaoh, "Let me leave, so I may go to my own country."

²² But Pharaoh asked him, "What do you lack here with me for you to want to go back to your own country?"

"Nothing," he replied, "but please let me leave."

²³ God raised up **Rezon** son of Eliada as an enemy against Solomon. Rezon had fled from his master King Hadadezer of Zobah ²⁴ and gathered men to himself. He became leader of a raiding party when David killed the Zobaites. He went to Damascus, lived there, and became king in Damascus. ²⁵ Rezon was Israel's enemy throughout Solomon's reign, adding to the trouble Hadad had caused. He reigned over Aram and loathed Israel.

²⁶ Now Solomon's servant, Jeroboam son of Nebat, was an Ephraimite from Zeredah. His widowed mother's name was Zeruah. Jeroboam rebelled against Solomon, ²⁷ and this is the reason he rebelled against the king: Solomon had built the supporting terraces and repaired the opening in the wall of the city of his father David. ²⁸ Now the man Jeroboam was capable, and Solomon noticed the young man because he was getting things done. So he appointed him over the entire labor force of the house of Joseph.

²⁹ During that time, the prophet Ahijah the Shilonite met Jeroboam on the road as Jeroboam came out of Jerusalem. Now Ahijah had wrapped himself with a new cloak, and the two of them were alone in the open field. ³⁰ Then Ahijah took hold of the new cloak he had on, tore it into twelve pieces, ³¹ and said to Jeroboam, "Take ten pieces for yourself, for this is what the LORD God of Israel says: 'I am about to tear the kingdom out of Solomon's hand. I will give you ten tribes, ³² but one tribe will remain his for the sake of my servant David and for the sake of Jerusalem, the city I chose out of all the tribes of Israel. ³³ For they have abandoned me; they have bowed down to Ashtoreth, the goddess of the Sidonians, to Chemosh, the god of Moab, and to Milcom, the god of the Ammonites. They have not walked in my ways to do what is right in my sight and to carry out my statutes and my judgments as his father David did.

³⁵ **I will take ten tribes of the kingdom from his son and give them to you.** ³⁷ **I will appoint you, and you will reign as king over all you want, and you will be king over Israel.**

⁴⁰ Therefore, Solomon tried to kill Jeroboam, but he fled to Egypt, to **King Shishak** of Egypt, where he remained until Solomon's death.

SOLOMON'S DEATH

⁴¹ The rest of the events of Solomon's reign, along with all his accomplishments and his wisdom, are written in the Book of Solomon's Events. ⁴² The length of Solomon's reign in Jerusalem over all Israel totaled forty years. ⁴³ Solomon rested with his fathers and was buried in the city of his father David. His son Rehoboam became king in his place.

Matthew 1:1–16
THE GENEALOGY OF JESUS CHRIST

¹ An account of the genealogy of Jesus Christ, the Son of David, the Son of Abraham:

FROM ABRAHAM TO DAVID

² Abraham fathered Isaac,
Isaac fathered Jacob,
Jacob fathered Judah and his brothers,
³ Judah fathered Perez and Zerah by Tamar,
Perez fathered Hezron,
Hezron fathered Aram,

⁴ Aram fathered Amminadab,
Amminadab fathered Nahshon,
Nahshon fathered Salmon,
⁵ Salmon fathered Boaz by Rahab,
Boaz fathered Obed by Ruth,
Obed fathered Jesse,
⁶ and Jesse fathered King David.

FROM DAVID TO THE BABYLONIAN EXILE

David fathered Solomon by Uriah's wife,
⁷ Solomon fathered Rehoboam,
Rehoboam fathered Abijah,
Abijah fathered Asa,
⁸ Asa fathered Jehoshaphat,
Jehoshaphat fathered Joram,
Joram fathered Uzziah,
⁹ Uzziah fathered Jotham,
Jotham fathered Ahaz,
Ahaz fathered Hezekiah,
¹⁰ Hezekiah fathered Manasseh,
Manasseh fathered Amon,
Amon fathered Josiah,
¹¹ and Josiah fathered Jeconiah and his brothers at the time of the exile to Babylon.

FROM THE EXILE TO THE CHRIST

¹² After the exile to Babylon
Jeconiah fathered Shealtiel,
Shealtiel fathered Zerubbabel,
¹³ Zerubbabel fathered Abiud,
Abiud fathered Eliakim,
Eliakim fathered Azor,
¹⁴ Azor fathered Zadok,
Zadok fathered Achim,
Achim fathered Eliud,
¹⁵ Eliud fathered Eleazar,
Eleazar fathered Matthan,
Matthan fathered Jacob,
¹⁶ and Jacob fathered Joseph the husband of Mary, who gave birth to Jesus who is called the Christ.

NOTES

*Solomon did what was evil in the L**ord**'s sight, and unlike his father David, he did not remain loyal to the L**ord**.*

I KINGS 11:6

Grace Day

DAY 6   Use this day to pray, rest, and reflect on this week's
          reading, giving thanks for the grace that is ours in Christ.

Now if any of you lacks wisdom,
he should ask God–who gives to
all generously and ungrudgingly–
and it will be given to him.

JAMES 1:5

DATE _____

W
E
E
K
L
Y

DAY · · · 7

T
R
U
T
H

Scripture is God-breathed and true. When we memorize it, we carry the gospel with us wherever we go.

This week we will memorize a portion of 1 Kings 2:4, when King David told Solomon of God's covenant and the purpose of the kings.

Find the corresponding memory card in the back of this book.

"If your sons guard their way to walk faithfully before me with all their heart and all their soul, you will never fail to have a man on the throne of Israel."

1 KINGS 2:4b

The Kingdom Divided

1 Kings 12

THE KINGDOM DIVIDED

¹ Then Rehoboam went to Shechem, for all Israel had gone to Shechem to make him king. ² When Jeroboam son of Nebat heard about it, he stayed in Egypt, where he had fled from King Solomon's presence. Jeroboam stayed in Egypt. ³ But they summoned him, and Jeroboam and the whole assembly of Israel came and spoke to Rehoboam: ⁴ "Your father made our yoke harsh. You, therefore, lighten your father's harsh service and the heavy yoke he put on us, and we will serve you."

⁵ Rehoboam replied, "Go away for three days and then return to me." So the people left. ⁶ Then King Rehoboam consulted with the elders who had served his father Solomon when he was alive, asking, "How do you advise me to respond to this people?"

⁷ They replied, "Today if you will be a servant to this people and serve them, and if you respond to them by speaking kind words to them, they will be your servants forever."

⁸ But he rejected the advice of the elders who had advised him and consulted with the young men who had grown up with him and attended him. ⁹ He asked them, "What message do you advise that we send back to this people who said to me, 'Lighten the yoke your father put on us'?"

¹⁰ Then the young men who had grown up with him told him, "This is what you should say to this people who said to you, 'Your father made our yoke heavy, but you, make it lighter on us!' This is what you should tell them: 'My little finger is thicker than my father's waist! ¹¹ Although my father burdened you with a heavy yoke, I will add to your yoke; my father disciplined you with whips, but I will discipline you with barbed whips.'"

¹² So Jeroboam and all the people came to Rehoboam on the third day, as the king had ordered: "Return to me on the third day." ¹³ Then the king answered the people harshly. He rejected the advice the elders had given him ¹⁴ and spoke to them according to the young men's advice: "My father made your yoke heavy, but I will add to your yoke; my father disciplined you with whips, but I will discipline you with barbed whips."

¹⁵ The king did not listen to the people, because this turn of events came from the LORD to carry out his word, which the LORD had spoken through Ahijah the Shilonite to Jeroboam son of Nebat. ¹⁶ When all Israel saw that the king had not listened to them, the people answered him:

> What portion do we have in David?
> We have no inheritance in the son of Jesse.
> Israel, return to your tents;
> David, now look after your own house!

So Israel went to their tents, [17] but Rehoboam reigned over the Israelites living in the cities of Judah.

[18] Then King Rehoboam sent Adoram, who was in charge of forced labor, but all Israel stoned him to death. King Rehoboam managed to get into the chariot and flee to Jerusalem. [19] Israel is still in rebellion against the house of David today.

REHOBOAM IN JERUSALEM

[20] When all Israel heard that Jeroboam had come back, they summoned him to the assembly and made him king over all Israel. No one followed the house of David except the tribe of Judah alone. [21] When Rehoboam arrived in Jerusalem, he mobilized one hundred eighty thousand fit young soldiers from the entire house of Judah and the tribe of Benjamin to fight against the house of Israel to restore the kingdom to Rehoboam son of Solomon. [22] But the word of God came to Shemaiah, the man of God: [23] "Say to Rehoboam son of Solomon, king of Judah, to the whole house of Judah and Benjamin, and to the rest of the people, [24] 'This is what the Lord says: You are not to march up and fight against your brothers, the Israelites. Each of you return home, for this situation is from me.'"

So they listened to the word of the Lord and went back according to the word of the Lord.

JEROBOAM'S IDOLATRY

[25] Jeroboam built Shechem in the hill country of Ephraim and lived there. From there he went out and built Penuel. [26] Jeroboam said to himself, "The kingdom might now return to the house of David. [27] If these people regularly go to offer sacrifices in the Lord's temple in Jerusalem, the heart of these people will return to their lord, King Rehoboam of Judah. They will kill me and go back to the king of Judah." [28] So the king sought advice.

Then he made two golden calves, and he said to the people, "Going to Jerusalem is too difficult for you. Israel, here are your gods who brought you up from the land of Egypt." [29] He set up one in Bethel, and put the other in Dan. [30] This led to sin; the people walked in procession before one of the calves all the way to Dan.

[31] Jeroboam also made shrines on the high places and made priests from the ranks of the people who were not Levites. [32] Jeroboam made a festival in the eighth month on the fifteenth day of the month, like the festival in Judah. He offered sacrifices on the altar; he made this offering in Bethel to sacrifice to the calves he had made.

No one followed the house of David except the tribe of Judah alone.

1 KINGS 12:20

He also stationed the priests in Bethel for the high places he had made. ³³ He offered sacrifices on the altar he had set up in Bethel on the fifteenth day of the eighth month. He chose this month on his own. He made a festival for the Israelites, offered sacrifices on the altar, and burned incense.

1 Kings 13

JUDGMENT ON JEROBOAM

¹ A man of God came, however, from Judah to Bethel by the word of the LORD while Jeroboam was standing beside the altar to burn incense. ² The man of God cried out against the altar by the word of the LORD: "Altar, altar, this is what the LORD says, 'A son will be born to the house of David, named Josiah, and he will sacrifice on you the priests of the high places who are burning incense on you. Human bones will be burned on you.'" ³ He gave a sign that day. He said, "This is the sign that the LORD has spoken: 'The altar will now be ripped apart, and the ashes that are on it will be poured out.'"

⁴ When the king heard the message that the man of God had cried out against the altar at Bethel, Jeroboam stretched out his hand from the altar and said, "Arrest him!" But the hand he stretched out against him withered, and he could not pull it back to himself. ⁵ The altar was ripped apart, and the ashes poured from the altar, according to the sign that the man of God had given by the word of the LORD.

⁶ Then the king responded to the man of God, "Plead for the favor of the LORD your God and pray for me so that my hand may be restored to me." So the man of God pleaded for the favor of the LORD, and the king's hand was restored to him and became as it had been at first.

⁷ Then the king declared to the man of God, "Come home with me, refresh yourself, and I'll give you a reward."

⁸ But the man of God replied, "If you were to give me half your house, I still wouldn't go with you, and I wouldn't eat food or drink water in this place, ⁹ for this is what I was commanded by the word of the LORD: 'You must not eat food or drink water or go back the way you came.'" ¹⁰ So he went another way; he did not go back by the way he had come to Bethel.

THE OLD PROPHET AND THE MAN OF GOD

¹¹ Now a certain old prophet was living in Bethel. His son came and told him all the deeds that the man of God had done that day in Bethel. His sons also told their father the words that he had spoken to the king. ¹² Then their father asked them, "Which way did he go?" His sons had seen the way taken by the man of God who had come from Judah. ¹³ Then he said to his sons, "Saddle the donkey for me." So they saddled the donkey for him, and he got on it. ¹⁴ He followed the man of God and found him sitting under an oak tree. He asked him, "Are you the man of God who came from Judah?"

"I am," he said.

¹⁵ Then he said to him, "Come home with me and eat some food."

¹⁶ But he answered, "I cannot go back with you or accompany you; I will not eat food or drink water with you in this place. ¹⁷ For a message came to me by the word of the LORD: 'You must not eat food or drink water there or go back by the way you came.'"

¹⁸ He said to him, "I am also a prophet like you. An angel spoke to me by the word of the LORD: 'Bring him back with you to your house so that he may eat food and drink water.'" The old prophet deceived him, ¹⁹ and the man of God went back with him, ate food in his house, and drank water.

²⁰ While they were sitting at the table, the word of the LORD came to the prophet who had brought him back, ²¹ and the prophet cried out to the man of God who had come from Judah, "This is what the LORD says: 'Because you rebelled against the LORD's command and did not keep the command that the LORD your God commanded you— ²² but you went back and ate food and drank water in the place that he said to you, "Do not eat food and do not drink water"—your corpse will never reach the grave of your fathers.'"

²³ So after he had eaten food and after he had drunk, the old prophet saddled the donkey for the prophet he had brought back. ²⁴ When he left, a lion attacked him along the way and killed him. His corpse was thrown on the road, and the

donkey was standing beside it; the lion was standing beside the corpse too.

25 There were men passing by who saw the corpse thrown on the road and the lion standing beside it, and they went and spoke about it in the city where the old prophet lived. 26 When the prophet who had brought him back from his way heard about it, he said, "He is the man of God who disobeyed the LORD's command. The LORD has given him to the lion, and it has mauled and killed him, according to the word of the LORD that he spoke to him."

27 Then the old prophet instructed his sons, "Saddle the donkey for me." They saddled it, 28 and he went and found the corpse thrown on the road with the donkey and the lion standing beside the corpse. The lion had not eaten the corpse or mauled the donkey. 29 So the prophet lifted the corpse of the man of God and laid it on the donkey and brought it back. The old prophet came into the city to mourn and to bury him. 30 Then he laid the corpse in his own grave, and they mourned over him: "Oh, my brother!"

31 After he had buried him, he said to his sons, "When I die, bury me in the grave where the man of God is buried; lay my bones beside his bones, 32 for the message that he cried out by the word of the LORD against the altar in Bethel and against all the shrines of the high places in the cities of Samaria is certain to happen."

33 Even after this, Jeroboam did not repent of his evil way but again made priests for the high places from the ranks of the people. He ordained whoever so desired it, and they became priests of the high places. 34 This was the sin that caused the house of Jeroboam to be cut off and obliterated from the face of the earth.

1 Kings 14:1–20

DISASTER ON THE HOUSE OF JEROBOAM

1 At that time Abijah son of Jeroboam became sick. 2 Jeroboam said to his wife, "Go disguise yourself, so they won't know that you're Jeroboam's wife, and go to Shiloh. The prophet Ahijah is there; it was he who told about me becoming king over this people. 3 Take with you ten loaves of bread, some cakes, and a jar of honey, and go to him. He will tell you what will happen to the boy."

4 Jeroboam's wife did that: she went to Shiloh and arrived at Ahijah's house. Ahijah could not see; he was blind due to his age. 5 But the LORD had said to Ahijah, "Jeroboam's wife is coming soon to ask you about her son, for he is sick. You are to say such and such to her. When she arrives, she will be disguised."

6 When Ahijah heard the sound of her feet entering the door, he said, "Come in, wife of Jeroboam! Why are you disguised? I have bad news for you. 7 Go tell Jeroboam, 'This is what the LORD God of Israel says: I raised you up from among the people, appointed you ruler over my people Israel, 8 tore the kingdom away from the house of David, and gave it to you. But you were not like my servant David, who kept my commands and followed me with all his heart, doing only what is right in my sight. 9 You behaved more wickedly than all who were before you. In order to anger me, you have proceeded to make for yourself other gods and cast images, but you have flung me behind your back. 10 Because of all this, I am about to bring disaster on the house of Jeroboam:

> I will wipe out all of Jeroboam's males,
> both slave and free, in Israel;
> I will sweep away the house of Jeroboam
> as one sweeps away dung until it is all gone!
> 11 Anyone who belongs to Jeroboam and dies in the city,
> the dogs will eat,
> and anyone who dies in the field,
> the birds will eat,
> for the LORD has spoken!'

12 "As for you, get up and go to your house. When your feet enter the city, the boy will die. 13 All Israel will mourn for him and bury him. He alone out of Jeroboam's house will be given a proper burial because out of the house of Jeroboam something favorable to the LORD God of Israel was found in him. 14 The LORD will raise up for himself a king over Israel, who will wipe out the house of Jeroboam. This is the day, yes, even today! 15 For the LORD will strike Israel so that they will shake as a reed shakes in water. He will uproot Israel from this good soil that he gave to their ancestors. He will scatter

them beyond the Euphrates because they made their **Asherah** poles, angering the LORD. [16] He will give up Israel because of Jeroboam's sins that he committed and caused Israel to commit."

[17] Then Jeroboam's wife got up and left and went to Tirzah. As she was crossing the threshold of the house, the boy died. [18] He was buried, and all Israel mourned for him, according to the word of the LORD he had spoken through his servant the prophet Ahijah.

[19] As for the rest of the events of Jeroboam's reign, how he waged war and how he reigned, note that they are written in the Historical Record of Israel's Kings. [20] The length of Jeroboam's reign was twenty-two years. He rested with his fathers, and his son Nadab became king in his place.

Ephesians 4:1–6

UNITY AND DIVERSITY IN THE BODY OF CHRIST

[1] Therefore I, the prisoner in the Lord, urge you to live worthy of the calling you have received, [2] with all humility and gentleness, with patience, bearing with one another in love, [3] making every effort to keep the unity of the Spirit through the bond of peace. [4] There is one body and one Spirit—just as you were called to one hope at your calling— [5] one Lord, one faith, one baptism, [6] one God and Father of all, who is above all and through all and in all.

Neighbors of Israel and Judah

PHOENICIA

DAN

SIDON

ARAM

TYRE

Sea of Galilee

JEZREEL

JABESH-GILEAD

Mediterranean Sea

TIRZAH

SAMARIA

SHECHEM

ISRAEL

Jordan River

AMMON

BETHEL

JERICHO

JERUSALEM

BETHLEHEM

HEBRON

Dead Sea

JUDAH

MOAB

BEERSHEBA

PHILISTIA

King's
Highway

Coastal
Highway

| O MI | IO | 20 | 30 | 40 |

| O KM | 20 | 40 | 60 |

TAMAR

EDOM

N

Ammonites

Descended from Abraham's nephew Lot (Gn 19:38). One of many people groups who persecuted Israel during the period of the judges (Jdg 11:4–33). Subdued by Israel during King David's reign (2Sm 8:12).

⚲ AMMON

KEY DEITIES
Milcom/Molech

KEY REFERENCES
1Kg 11:1–8, 33;
2Kg 23:10–14; 24:2

Amorites

Sometimes used to refer to multiple people groups in Canaan

Among the original inhabitants of Canaan before the Israelites' conquest (Nm 21:21–35). Forced to become part of King Solomon's workforce.

KEY REFERENCES
1Kg 9:20–21; 21:25–26;
2Kg 21:11

Arameans

Also known as Syrians

Descendants of Aram, grandson of Noah (Gn 10:21–22). Regularly warred against Israel during King David's reign (2Sm 10:15–19).

⚲ ARAM

KEY PEOPLE
Rezon, King Ben-hadad, King Hazael, Naaman, King Rezin

KEY DEITIES
Ashtoreth, Rimmon, Ashima

KEY REFERENCES
1Kg 20:1–34; 22:1–36;
2Kg 6:8–7:20

Assyrians

People from one of the most powerful kingdoms in the ancient Near East. Invaded and conquered the northern kingdom of Israel in 722 BC, sending the Israelites into exile.

KEY PEOPLE
King Tiglath-pileser, King Shalmaneser, King Sennacherib

KEY DEITIES
Nibhaz, Tartak

KEY REFERENCES
2Kg 15:17–20; 17–19;
20:4–6

Babylonians

Also known as Chaldeans

Supplanted the Assyrians to become the dominant power in the ancient world. Conquered Judah and exiled its people in 586 BC.

KEY PEOPLE
King Merodach-baladan, King Nebuchadnezzar, Nebuzaradan, King Evil-marodach

KEY DEITIES
Succoth-benoth, Nergal

KEY REFERENCES
2Kg 17:24, 30; 24–25

Canaanites

Sometimes used to refer to multiple people groups in Canaan

Descendants of Noah's grandson Canaan (Gn 10:6). Inhabited the land of Canaan prior to the conquest and into the period of the monarchy.

KEY DEITIES
Asherah, Ashtoreth, Baal, Milcom/Molech

KEY REFERENCES
2Kg 10:18–28; 17:10–16

Edomites

Descendants of Abraham's grandson Esau (Gn 25:30). Warred against both King Saul and King David (1Sm 14:47).

⚲ EDOM

KEY PEOPLE
King Hadad

KEY REFERENCES
1Kg 11:1–16; 2Kg 8:20–22

Egyptians

Descendants of Noah's grandson Mizraim (Gn 10:6). Enslaved the Israelite people in the land of Egypt (Ex 12:40).

KEY PEOPLE
Pharaoh (unnamed), Queen Tahpenes, King Shishak, Pharaoh Neco

KEY REFERENCES
1Kg 9:16; 14:25–26; 2Kg 23:29

Midianites

Descendants of Abraham's son Midian by his second wife, Keturah (Gn 25:1–2). Welcomed Moses after he fled from Pharaoh (Ex 2:15). Oppressed Israel during the period of the judges (Jdg 6:1–8:21).

KEY REFERENCES
1Kg 11:18

Moabites

Descendants of Abraham's nephew Lot (Gn 19:37). Fought against Israel during the reigns of King Saul and King David (1Sm 14:47; 2Sm 8:2).

⚲ MOAB

KEY DEITIES
Chemosh, Baal

KEY REFERENCES
1Kg 11:1–7; 2Kg 3:4–27

Sepharvites

Sent to Israel to repopulate the land after the Assyrians conquered Israel in 722 BC. Known for practicing child sacrifice.

KEY DEITIES
Adrammelech, Anammelech

KEY REFERENCES
2Kg 17:24–41

Sidonians

Residents of the city of Sidon on the coast of the Mediterranean Sea, north of Israel. Home city of Queen Jezebel, wife of King Ahab.

KEY PEOPLE
Queen Jezebel

KEY DEITIES
Ashtoreth

KEY REFERENCES
1Kg 11:5–13; 16:31–33

Tyrians

Residents of the city of Tyre on the coast of the Mediterranean Sea, south of Sidon. Often cooperated with Israel.

KEY PEOPLE
King Hiram, Hiram the craftsman

KEY REFERENCES
1Kg 5:1–12; 9:12–13, 26–28

Judah and Israel's Kings

DAY

9

Rehoboam, Abijam, Asa, Nadab, Baasha, Elah, Zimri, Tibni, Omri, Ahab

Judah, Israel

1 Kings 14:21–31

JUDAH'S KING REHOBOAM

²¹ Now Rehoboam, Solomon's son, reigned in Judah. Rehoboam was forty-one years old when he became king; he reigned seventeen years in Jerusalem, the city where the LORD had chosen from all the tribes of Israel to put his name. Rehoboam's mother's name was Naamah the Ammonite.

²² Judah did what was evil in the LORD's sight. They provoked him to jealous anger more than all that their ancestors had done with the sins they committed. ²³ They also built for themselves high places, sacred pillars, and Asherah poles on every high hill and under every green tree; ²⁴ there were even male cult prostitutes in the land. They imitated all the detestable practices of the nations the LORD had dispossessed before the Israelites.

²⁵ In the fifth year of King Rehoboam, King Shishak of Egypt went to war against Jerusalem. ²⁶ He seized the treasuries of the LORD's temple and the treasuries of the royal palace. He took everything. He took all the gold shields that Solomon had made. ²⁷ King Rehoboam made bronze shields to replace them and committed them into the care of the captains of the guards who protected the entrance to the king's palace. ²⁸ Whenever the king entered the LORD's temple, the guards would carry the shields, then they would take them back to the armory.

²⁹ The rest of the events of Rehoboam's reign, along with all his accomplishments, are written about in the Historical Record of Judah's Kings. ³⁰ There was war between Rehoboam and Jeroboam throughout their reigns. ³¹ Rehoboam rested with his fathers and was buried with his fathers in the city of David. His mother's name was Naamah the Ammonite. His son Abijam became king in his place.

1 Kings 15

JUDAH'S KING ABIJAM

¹ In the eighteenth year of Israel's King Jeroboam son of Nebat, Abijam became king over Judah, ² and he reigned three years in Jerusalem. His mother's name was Maacah daughter of Abishalom.

³ Abijam walked in all the sins his father before him had committed, and he was not wholeheartedly devoted to the LORD his God as his ancestor David had been. ⁴ But for the sake of David, the LORD his God gave him a lamp in Jerusalem by raising up his son after him and by preserving Jerusalem. ⁵ For David did what was right in the LORD's sight, and he did not turn aside from anything he had commanded him all the days of his life, except in the matter of Uriah the Hethite.

⁶ There had been war between Rehoboam and Jeroboam all the days of Rehoboam's life. ⁷ The rest of the events of Abijam's reign, along with all his accomplishments, are written in the Historical Record of Judah's Kings. There was also war between Abijam and Jeroboam. ⁸ Abijam rested with his fathers and was buried in the city of David. His son Asa became king in his place.

JUDAH'S KING ASA

⁹ In the twentieth year of Israel's King Jeroboam, Asa became king of Judah, ¹⁰ and he reigned forty-one years in Jerusalem. His grandmother's name was Maacah daughter of Abishalom.

¹¹ Asa did what was right in the LORD's sight, as his ancestor David had done. ¹² He banished the male cult prostitutes from the land and removed all of the idols that his fathers had made. ¹³ He also removed his grandmother Maacah from being queen mother because she had made an obscene image of Asherah. Asa chopped down her obscene image and burned it in the Kidron Valley. ¹⁴ The high places were not taken away, but Asa was wholeheartedly devoted to the LORD his entire life. ¹⁵ He brought his father's consecrated gifts and his own consecrated gifts into the LORD's temple: silver, gold, and utensils.

¹⁶ There was war between Asa and King Baasha of Israel throughout their reigns. ¹⁷ Israel's King Baasha went to war against Judah. He built Ramah in order to keep anyone from leaving or coming to King Asa of Judah. ¹⁸ So Asa withdrew all the silver and gold that remained in the treasuries of the LORD's temple and the treasuries of the royal palace and gave it to his servants. Then King Asa sent them to Ben-hadad son of Tabrimmon son of Hezion king of Aram who lived in Damascus, saying, ¹⁹ "There is a treaty between me and you, between my father and your father. Look, I have sent you a gift of silver and gold. Go and break your treaty with King Baasha of Israel so that he will withdraw from me."

²⁰ Ben-hadad listened to King Asa and sent the commanders of his armies against the cities of Israel. He attacked Ijon, Dan, Abel-beth-maacah, all Chinnereth, and the whole land of Naphtali. ²¹ When Baasha heard about it, he quit building Ramah and stayed in Tirzah. ²² Then King Asa gave a command to everyone without exception in Judah, and they carried away the stones of Ramah and the timbers Baasha had built it with. Then King Asa built Geba of Benjamin and Mizpah with them.

²³ The rest of all the events of Asa's reign, along with all his might, all his accomplishments, and the cities he built, are written in the Historical Record of Judah's Kings. But in his old age he developed a disease in his feet. ²⁴ Then Asa rested with his fathers and was buried in the city of his ancestor David. His son Jehoshaphat became king in his place.

ISRAEL'S KING NADAB

²⁵ Nadab son of Jeroboam became king over Israel in the second year of Judah's King Asa; he reigned over Israel two years. ²⁶ Nadab did what was evil in the LORD's sight and walked in the ways of his father and the sin he had caused Israel to commit.

²⁷ Then Baasha son of Ahijah of the house of Issachar conspired against Nadab, and Baasha struck him down at Gibbethon of the Philistines while Nadab and all Israel were besieging Gibbethon. ²⁸ In the third year of Judah's King Asa, Baasha killed Nadab and reigned in his place.

²⁹ When Baasha became king, he struck down the entire house of Jeroboam. He did not leave Jeroboam any survivors but destroyed his family according to the word of the LORD he had spoken through his servant Ahijah the Shilonite. ³⁰ This was because Jeroboam had angered the LORD God of Israel by the sins he had committed and had caused Israel to commit.

³¹ The rest of the events of Nadab's reign, along with all his accomplishments, are written in the Historical Record of Israel's Kings. ³² There was war between Asa and King Baasha of Israel throughout their reigns.

ISRAEL'S KING BAASHA

³³ In the third year of Judah's King Asa, Baasha son of Ahijah became king over all Israel, and he reigned in Tirzah twenty-four years. ³⁴ He did what was evil in the LORD's sight and walked in the ways of Jeroboam and the sin he had caused Israel to commit.

[1] Now the word of the LORD came to Jehu son of Hanani against Baasha: [2] "Because I raised you up from the dust and made you ruler over my people Israel, but you have walked in the ways of Jeroboam and have caused my people Israel to sin, angering me with their sins, [3] take note: I will eradicate Baasha and his house, and I will make your house like the house of Jeroboam son of Nebat:

[4] Anyone who belongs to Baasha and dies in the city,
the dogs will eat,
and anyone who is his and dies in the field,
the birds will eat."

[5] The rest of the events of Baasha's reign, along with all his accomplishments and might, are written in the Historical Record of Israel's Kings. [6] Baasha rested with his fathers and was buried in Tirzah. His son Elah became king in his place. [7] But through the prophet Jehu son of Hanani the word of the LORD also had come against Baasha and against his house because of all the evil he had done in the LORD's sight. His actions angered the LORD, and Baasha's house became like the house of Jeroboam, because he had struck it down.

ISRAEL'S KING ELAH

[8] In the twenty-sixth year of Judah's King Asa, Elah son of Baasha became king over Israel, and he reigned in Tirzah two years.

[9] His servant Zimri, commander of half his chariots, conspired against him while Elah was in Tirzah getting drunk in the house of Arza, who was in charge of the household at Tirzah. [10] In the twenty-seventh year of Judah's King Asa, Zimri went in, struck Elah down, killing him. Then Zimri became king in his place.

[11] When he became king, as soon as he was seated on his throne, Zimri struck down the entire house of Baasha. He did not leave a single male, including his kinsmen and his friends. [12] So Zimri destroyed the entire house of Baasha, according to the word of the LORD he had spoken against Baasha through the prophet Jehu. [13] This happened because of all the sins of Baasha and those of his son Elah, which they committed and caused Israel to commit, angering the LORD God of Israel with their worthless idols.

[14] The rest of the events of Elah's reign, along with all his accomplishments, are written in the Historical Record of Israel's Kings.

ISRAEL'S KING ZIMRI

[15] In the twenty-seventh year of Judah's King Asa, Zimri became king for seven days in Tirzah. Now the troops were encamped against Gibbethon of the Philistines. [16] When these troops heard that Zimri had not only conspired but had

also struck down the king, then all Israel made Omri, the army commander, king over Israel that very day in the camp. [17] Omri along with all Israel marched up from Gibbethon and besieged Tirzah. [18] When Zimri saw that the city was captured, he entered the citadel of the royal palace and burned it down over himself. He died [19] because of the sin he committed by doing what was evil in the LORD's sight and by walking in the ways of Jeroboam and the sin he caused Israel to commit.

[20] The rest of the events of Zimri's reign, along with the conspiracy that he instigated, are written in the Historical Record of Israel's Kings. [21] At that time the people of Israel were divided: half the people followed Tibni son of Ginath, to make him king, and half followed Omri. [22] However, the people who followed Omri proved stronger than those who followed Tibni son of Ginath. So Tibni died and Omri became king.

ISRAEL'S KING OMRI

[23] In the thirty-first year of Judah's King Asa, Omri became king over Israel, and he reigned twelve years. He reigned six years in Tirzah, [24] then he bought the hill of Samaria from Shemer for 150 pounds of silver, and he built up the hill. He named the city he built Samaria based on the name Shemer, the owner of the hill.

[25] Omri did what was evil in the LORD's sight; he did more evil than all who were before him. [26] He walked in all the ways of Jeroboam son of Nebat in every respect and continued in his sins that he caused Israel to commit, angering the LORD God of Israel with their worthless idols. [27] The rest of the events of Omri's reign, along with his accomplishments and the might he exercised, are written in the Historical Record of Israel's Kings. [28] Omri rested with his fathers and was buried in Samaria. His son Ahab became king in his place.

ISRAEL'S KING AHAB

[29] Ahab son of Omri became king over Israel in the thirty-eighth year of Judah's King Asa; Ahab son of Omri reigned over Israel in Samaria twenty-two years. [30] But Ahab son of Omri did what was evil in the LORD's sight more than all who were before him. [31] Then, as if following the sin of Jeroboam son of Nebat were not enough, he married

Jezebel, the daughter of Ethbaal king of the Sidonians, and then proceeded to serve **Baal** and bow in worship to him. [32] He set up an altar for Baal in the temple of Baal that he had built in Samaria. [33] Ahab also made an Asherah pole. Ahab did more to anger the LORD God of Israel than all the kings of Israel who were before him.

[34] During his reign, Hiel the Bethelite built Jericho. At the cost of Abiram his firstborn, he laid its foundation, and at the cost of Segub his youngest, he finished its gates, according to the word of the LORD he had spoken through Joshua son of Nun.

2 Samuel 7:14–17

[14] "'I will be his father, and he will be my son. When he does wrong, I will discipline him with a rod of men and blows from mortals. [15] But my faithful love will never leave him as it did when I removed it from Saul, whom I removed from before you. [16] Your house and kingdom will endure before me forever, and your throne will be established forever.'"

[17] Nathan reported all these words and this entire vision to David.

Isaiah 41:28–29

[28] "When I look, there is no one;
there is no counselor among them;
when I ask them, they have nothing to say.
[29] Look, all of them are a delusion;
their works are nonexistent;
their images are wind and emptiness."

·

NOTES

But for the sake of David, the Lᴏʀᴅ his God gave him a lamp in Jerusalem by raising up
his son after him and by preserving Jerusalem.

1 KINGS 15:4

The Ministry of Elijah

1 Kings 17

ELIJAH ANNOUNCES FAMINE

¹ Now Elijah the Tishbite, from the Gilead settlers, said to Ahab, "As the LORD God of Israel lives, in whose presence I stand, there will be no dew or rain during these years except by my command!"

² Then the word of the LORD came to him: ³ "Leave here, turn eastward, and hide at the Wadi Cherith where it enters the Jordan. ⁴ You are to drink from the wadi. I have commanded the ravens to provide for you there."

⁵ So he proceeded to do what the LORD commanded. Elijah left and lived at the Wadi Cherith where it enters the Jordan. ⁶ The ravens kept bringing him bread and meat in the morning and in the evening, and he would drink from the wadi. ⁷ After a while, the wadi dried up because there had been no rain in the land.

ELIJAH AND THE WIDOW

⁸ Then the word of the LORD came to him: ⁹ "Get up, go to Zarephath that belongs to Sidon and stay there. Look, I have commanded a woman who is a widow to provide for you there." ¹⁰ So Elijah got up and went to Zarephath. When he arrived at the city gate, there was a widow gathering wood. Elijah called to her and said, "Please bring me a little water in a cup and let me drink." ¹¹ As she went to get it, he called to her and said, "Please bring me a piece of bread in your hand."

¹² But she said, "As the LORD your God lives, I don't have anything baked—only a handful of flour in the jar and a bit of oil in the jug. Just now, I am gathering a couple of sticks in order to go prepare it for myself and my son so we can eat it and die."

¹³ Then Elijah said to her, "Don't be afraid; go and do as you have said. But first make me a small loaf from it and bring it out to me. Afterward, you may make some for yourself and your son, ¹⁴ for this is what the LORD God of Israel says, 'The flour jar will not become empty and the oil jug will not run dry until the day the LORD sends rain on the surface of the land.'"

¹⁵ So she proceeded to do according to the word of Elijah. Then the woman, Elijah, and her household ate for many days. ¹⁶ The flour jar did not become empty, and the oil jug did not run dry, according to the word of the LORD he had spoken through Elijah.

Now I know you are a man of God and the Lord's word from your mouth is true.

1 KINGS 17:24

THE WIDOW'S SON RAISED

[17] After this, the son of the woman who owned the house became ill. His illness got worse until he stopped breathing. [18] She said to Elijah, "Man of God, why are you here? Have you come to call attention to my iniquity so that my son is put to death?"

[19] But Elijah said to her, "Give me your son." So he took him from her arms, brought him up to the upstairs room where he was staying, and laid him on his own bed. [20] Then he cried out to the LORD and said, "LORD my God, have you also brought tragedy on the widow I am staying with by killing her son?" [21] Then he stretched himself out over the boy three times. He cried out to the LORD and said, "LORD my God, please let this boy's life come into him again!"

[22] So the LORD listened to Elijah, and the boy's life came into him again, and he lived. [23] Then Elijah took the boy, brought him down from the upstairs room into the house, and gave him to his mother. Elijah said, "Look, your son is alive."

[24] Then the woman said to Elijah, "Now I know you are a man of God and the LORD's word from your mouth is true."

1 Kings 18

ELIJAH'S MESSAGE TO AHAB

[1] After a long time, the word of the LORD came to Elijah in the third year: "Go and present yourself to Ahab. I will send rain on the surface of the land." [2] So Elijah went to present himself to Ahab.

The famine was severe in Samaria. [3] Ahab called for Obadiah, who was in charge of the palace. Obadiah was a man who greatly feared the LORD [4] and took a hundred prophets and hid them, fifty men to a cave, and provided them with food and water when Jezebel slaughtered the LORD's prophets. [5] Ahab said to Obadiah, "Go throughout the land to every spring and to every wadi. Perhaps we'll find grass so we can keep the horses and mules alive and not have to destroy any cattle." [6] They divided the land between them in order to cover it. Ahab went one way by himself, and Obadiah went the other way by himself.

[7] While Obadiah was walking along the road, Elijah suddenly met him. When Obadiah recognized him, he fell facedown and said, "Is it you, my lord Elijah?"

[8] "It is I," he replied. "Go tell your lord, 'Elijah is here!'"

[9] But Obadiah said, "What sin have I committed, that you are handing your servant over to Ahab to put me to death? [10] As the LORD your God lives, there is no nation or kingdom where my lord has not sent someone to search for you. When

they said, 'He is not here,' he made that kingdom or nation swear they had not found you.

¹¹ "Now you say, 'Go tell your lord, "Elijah is here!"' ¹² But when I leave you, the Spirit of the LORD may carry you off to some place I don't know. Then when I go report to Ahab and he doesn't find you, he will kill me. But I, your servant, have feared the LORD from my youth. ¹³ Wasn't it reported to my lord what I did when Jezebel slaughtered the LORD's prophets? I hid a hundred of the prophets of the LORD, fifty men to a cave, and I provided them with food and water. ¹⁴ Now you say, 'Go tell your lord, "Elijah is here!"' He will kill me!"

¹⁵ Then Elijah said, "As the LORD of Armies lives, in whose presence I stand, today I will present myself to Ahab."

¹⁶ Obadiah went to meet Ahab and told him. Then Ahab went to meet Elijah. ¹⁷ When Ahab saw Elijah, Ahab said to him, "Is that you, the one ruining Israel?"

¹⁸ He replied, "I have not ruined Israel, but you and your father's family have, because you have abandoned the LORD's commands and followed the Baals. ¹⁹ Now summon all Israel to meet me at Mount Carmel, along with the 450 prophets of Baal and the 400 prophets of Asherah who eat at Jezebel's table."

ELIJAH AT MOUNT CARMEL

²⁰ So Ahab summoned all the Israelites and gathered the prophets at Mount Carmel. ²¹ Then Elijah approached all the people and said, "How long will you waver between two opinions? If the LORD is God, follow him. But if Baal, follow him." But the people didn't answer him a word.

²² Then Elijah said to the people, "I am the only remaining prophet of the LORD, but Baal's prophets are 450 men. ²³ Let two bulls be given to us. They are to choose one bull for themselves, cut it in pieces, and place it on the wood but not light the fire. I will prepare the other bull and place it on the wood but not light the fire. ²⁴ Then you call on the name of your god, and I will call on the name of the LORD. The God who answers with fire, he is God."

All the people answered, "That's fine."

²⁵ Then Elijah said to the prophets of Baal, "Since you are so numerous, choose for yourselves one bull and prepare it first. Then call on the name of your god but don't light the fire."

²⁶ So they took the bull that he gave them, prepared it, and called on the name of Baal from morning until noon, saying, "Baal, answer us!" But there was no sound; no one answered. Then they danced around the altar they had made.

²⁷ At noon Elijah mocked them. He said, "Shout loudly, for he's a god! Maybe he's thinking it over; maybe he has wandered away; or maybe he's on the road. Perhaps he's sleeping and will wake up!" ²⁸ They shouted loudly, and cut themselves with knives and spears, according to their custom, until blood gushed over them. ²⁹ All afternoon they kept on raving until the offering of the evening sacrifice, but there was no sound; no one answered, no one paid attention.

³⁰ Then Elijah said to all the people, "Come near me." So all the people approached him. Then he repaired the LORD's altar that had been torn down: ³¹ Elijah took twelve stones—according to the number of the tribes of the sons of Jacob, to whom the word of the LORD had come, saying, "Israel will be your name"— ³² and he built an altar with the stones in the name of the LORD. Then he made a trench around the altar large enough to hold about four gallons. ³³ Next, he arranged the wood, cut up the bull, and placed it on the wood. He said, "Fill four water pots with water and pour it on the offering to be burned and on the wood." ³⁴ Then he said, "A second time!" and they did it a second time. And then he said, "A third time!" and they did it a third time. ³⁵ So the water ran all around the altar; he even filled the trench with water.

³⁶ At the time for offering the evening sacrifice, the prophet Elijah approached the altar and said, "LORD, the God of Abraham, Isaac, and Israel, today let it be known that you are God in Israel and I am your servant, and that at your word I have done all these things. ³⁷ Answer me, LORD! Answer me so that this people will know that you, the LORD, are God and that you have turned their hearts back."

³⁸ Then the Lord's fire fell and consumed the burnt offering, the wood, the stones, and the dust, and it licked up the water that was in the trench. ³⁹ When all the people saw it, they fell facedown and said,

"The Lord, he is God! The Lord, he is God!"

⁴⁰ Then Elijah ordered them, "Seize the prophets of Baal! Do not let even one of them escape." So they seized them, and Elijah brought them down to the Wadi Kishon and slaughtered them there. ⁴¹ Elijah said to Ahab, "Go up, eat and drink, for there is the sound of a rainstorm."

⁴² So Ahab went to eat and drink, but Elijah went up to the summit of Carmel. He bent down on the ground and put his face between his knees. ⁴³ Then he said to his servant, "Go up and look toward the sea."

So he went up, looked, and said, "There's nothing."

Seven times Elijah said, "Go back."

⁴⁴ On the seventh time, he reported, "There's a cloud as small as a man's hand coming up from the sea."

Then Elijah said, "Go and tell Ahab, 'Get your chariot ready and go down so the rain doesn't stop you.'"

⁴⁵ In a little while, the sky grew dark with clouds and wind, and there was a downpour. So Ahab got in his chariot and went to Jezreel. ⁴⁶ The power of the Lord was on Elijah, and he tucked his mantle under his belt and ran ahead of Ahab to the entrance of Jezreel.

1 Kings 19

ELIJAH'S JOURNEY TO HOREB

¹ Ahab told Jezebel everything that Elijah had done and how he had killed all the prophets with the sword. ² So Jezebel sent a messenger to Elijah, saying, "May the gods punish me and do so severely if I don't make your life like the life of one of them by this time tomorrow!"

³ Then Elijah became afraid and immediately ran for his life. When he came to Beer-sheba that belonged to Judah, he left his servant there, ⁴ but he went on a day's journey into the wilderness. He sat down under a broom tree and prayed that he might die. He said, "I have had enough! Lord, take my life, for I'm no better than my fathers." ⁵ Then he lay down and slept under the broom tree.

Suddenly, an angel touched him. The angel told him, "Get up and eat." ⁶ Then he looked, and there at his head was a loaf of bread baked over hot stones, and a jug of water. So he ate and drank and lay down again. ⁷ Then the angel of the Lord returned for a second time and touched him. He said, "Get up and eat, or the journey will be too much for you." ⁸ So he got up, ate, and drank. Then on the strength from that food, he walked forty days and forty nights to Horeb, the mountain of God. ⁹ He entered a cave there and spent the night.

ELIJAH'S ENCOUNTER WITH THE LORD

Suddenly, the word of the Lord came to him, and he said to him, "What are you doing here, Elijah?"

¹⁰ He replied, "I have been very zealous for the Lord God of Armies, but the Israelites have abandoned your covenant, torn down your altars, and killed your prophets with the sword. I alone am left, and they are looking for me to take my life."

¹¹ Then he said, "Go out and stand on the mountain in the Lord's presence."

At that moment, the Lord passed by. A great and mighty wind was tearing at the mountains and was shattering cliffs before the Lord, but the Lord was not in the wind. After the wind there was an earthquake, but the Lord was not in the earthquake. ¹² After the earthquake there was a fire, but the Lord was not in the fire. And after the fire there was a voice, a soft whisper. ¹³ When Elijah heard it, he wrapped his face in his mantle and went out and stood at the entrance of the cave.

Suddenly, a voice came to him and said, "What are you doing here, Elijah?"

[14] "I have been very zealous for the LORD God of Armies," he replied, "but the Israelites have abandoned your covenant, torn down your altars, and killed your prophets with the sword. I alone am left, and they're looking for me to take my life."

[15] Then the LORD said to him, "Go and return by the way you came to the Wilderness of Damascus. When you arrive, you are to anoint **Hazael** as king over Aram. [16] You are to anoint Jehu son of Nimshi as king over Israel and Elisha son of Shaphat from Abel-meholah as prophet in your place. [17] Then Jehu will put to death whoever escapes the sword of Hazael, and Elisha will put to death whoever escapes the sword of Jehu. [18] But I will leave seven thousand in Israel—every knee that has not bowed to Baal and every mouth that has not kissed him."

ELISHA'S APPOINTMENT AS ELIJAH'S SUCCESSOR

[19] Elijah left there and found Elisha son of Shaphat as he was plowing. Twelve teams of oxen were in front of him, and he was with the twelfth team. Elijah walked by him and threw his mantle over him. [20] Elisha left the oxen, ran to follow Elijah, and said, "Please let me kiss my father and mother, and then I will follow you."

"Go on back," he replied, "for what have I done to you?"

[21] So he turned back from following him, took the team of oxen, and slaughtered them. With the oxen's wooden yoke and plow, he cooked the meat and gave it to the people, and they ate. Then he left, followed Elijah, and served him.

Joshua 6:26–27

[26] At that time Joshua imposed this curse:

> The man who undertakes
> the rebuilding of this city, Jericho,
> is cursed before the LORD.
> He will lay its foundation
> at the cost of his firstborn;
> he will finish its gates
> at the cost of his youngest.

[27] And the LORD was with Joshua, and his fame spread throughout the land.

Judgment on Ahab

1 Kings 20

VICTORY OVER BEN-HADAD

¹ Now **King Ben-hadad** of Aram assembled his entire army. Thirty-two kings, along with horses and chariots, were with him. He marched up, besieged Samaria, and fought against it. ² He sent messengers into the city to King Ahab of Israel and said to him, "This is what Ben-hadad says: ³ 'Your silver and your gold are mine! And your best wives and children are mine as well!'"

⁴ Then the king of Israel answered, "Just as you say, my lord the king: I am yours, along with all that I have."

⁵ The messengers then returned and said, "This is what Ben-hadad says: 'I have sent messengers to you, saying: You are to give me your silver, your gold, your wives, and your children. ⁶ But at this time tomorrow I will send my servants to you, and they will search your palace and your servants' houses. They will lay their hands on and take away whatever is precious to you.'"

⁷ Then the king of Israel called for all the elders of the land and said, "Recognize that this one is only looking for trouble, for he demanded my wives, my children, my silver, and my gold, and I didn't turn him down."

⁸ All the elders and all the people said to him, "Don't listen or agree."

⁹ So he said to Ben-hadad's messengers, "Say to my lord the king, 'Everything you demanded of your servant the first time, I will do, but this thing I cannot do.'" So the messengers left and took word back to him.

¹⁰ Then Ben-hadad sent messengers to him and said, "May the gods punish me and do so severely if Samaria's dust amounts to a handful for each of the people who follow me."

¹¹ The king of Israel answered, "Say this: 'Don't let the one who puts on his armor boast like the one who takes it off.'"

¹² When Ben-hadad heard this response, while he and the kings were drinking in their quarters, he said to his servants, "Take your positions." So they took their positions against the city.

¹³ A prophet approached King Ahab of Israel and said, "This is what the LORD says: 'Do you see this whole huge army? Watch, I am handing it over to you today so that you may know that I am the LORD.'"

¹⁴ Ahab asked, "By whom?"

And the prophet said, "This is what the LORD says: 'By the young men of the provincial leaders.'"

Then he asked, "Who is to start the battle?"

He said, "You."

¹⁵ So Ahab mobilized the young men of the provincial leaders, and there were 232. After them he mobilized all the Israelite troops: 7,000. ¹⁶ They marched out at noon while Ben-hadad and the thirty-two kings who were helping him were getting drunk in their quarters. ¹⁷ The young men of the provincial leaders marched out first. Then Ben-hadad sent out scouts, and they reported to him, saying, "Men are marching out of Samaria."

¹⁸ So he said, "If they have marched out in peace, take them alive, and if they have marched out for battle, take them alive."

¹⁹ The young men of the provincial leaders and the army behind them marched out from the city, ²⁰ and each one struck down his opponent. So the Arameans fled and Israel pursued them, but King Ben-hadad of Aram escaped on a horse with the cavalry. ²¹ Then the king of Israel marched out and attacked the cavalry and the chariots. He inflicted a severe slaughter on Aram.

²² The prophet approached the king of Israel and said to him, "Go and strengthen yourself, then consider carefully what you should do, for in the spring the king of Aram will attack you."

²³ Now the king of Aram's servants said to him, "Their gods are gods of the hill country. That's why they were stronger than we were. Instead, we should fight with them on the plain; then we will certainly be stronger than they are. ²⁴ Also do this: remove each king from his position and appoint captains in their place. ²⁵ Raise another army for yourself like the army you lost—horse for horse, chariot for chariot—and let's fight with them on the plain; and we will certainly be stronger than they are." The king listened to them and did it.

²⁶ In the spring, Ben-hadad mobilized the Arameans and went up to Aphek to battle Israel. ²⁷ The Israelites mobilized, gathered supplies, and went to fight them. The Israelites camped in front of them like two little flocks of goats, while the Arameans filled the landscape.

²⁸ Then the man of God approached and said to the king of Israel, "This is what the LORD says: 'Because the Arameans have said: The LORD is a god of the mountains and not a god of the valleys, I will hand over all this whole huge army to you. Then you will know that I am the LORD.'"

²⁹ They camped opposite each other for seven days. On the seventh day, the battle took place, and the Israelites struck down the Arameans—one hundred thousand foot soldiers in one day. ³⁰ The ones who remained fled into the city of Aphek, and the wall fell on those twenty-seven thousand remaining men.

Ben-hadad also fled and went into an inner room in the city. ³¹ His servants said to him, "Consider this: we have heard that the kings of the house of Israel are merciful kings. So let's put sackcloth around our waists and ropes around our heads, and let's go out to the king of Israel. Perhaps he will spare your life."

³² So they dressed with sackcloth around their waists and ropes around their heads, went to the king of Israel, and said, "Your servant Ben-hadad says, 'Please spare my life.'"

So he said, "Is he still alive? He is my brother."

³³ Now the men were looking for a sign of hope, so they quickly picked up on this and responded, "Yes, it is your brother Ben-hadad."

Then he said, "Go and bring him."

So Ben-hadad came out to him, and Ahab had him come up into the chariot. ³⁴ Then Ben-hadad said to him, "I restore to you the cities that my father took from your father, and you may set up marketplaces for yourself in Damascus, like my father set up in Samaria."

Ahab responded, "On the basis of this treaty, I release you." So he made a treaty with him and released him.

³⁵ One of the sons of the prophets said to his fellow prophet by the word of the LORD, "Strike me!" But the man refused to strike him.

³⁶ He told him, "Because you did not listen to the LORD, mark my words: When you leave me, a lion will kill you." When he left him, a lion attacked and killed him.

³⁷ The prophet found another man and said to him, "Strike me!" So the man struck him, inflicting a wound. ³⁸ Then the prophet went and waited for the king on the road. He disguised himself with a bandage over his eyes. ³⁹ As the king was passing by, he cried out to the king and said, "Your servant marched out into the middle of the battle. Suddenly, a man turned aside and brought someone to me and said, 'Guard this man! If he is ever missing, it will be your life in place of his life, or you will weigh out seventy-five pounds of silver.' ⁴⁰ But while your servant was busy here and there, he disappeared."

The king of Israel said to him, "That will be your sentence; you yourself have decided it."

⁴¹ He quickly removed the bandage from his eyes. The king of Israel recognized that he was one of the prophets. ⁴² The prophet said to him, "This is what the LORD says: 'Because you released from your hand the man I had set apart for destruction, it will be your life in place of his life and your people in place of his people.'" ⁴³ The king of Israel left for home resentful and angry, and he entered Samaria.

1 Kings 21

AHAB AND NABOTH'S VINEYARD

¹ Some time passed after these events. Naboth the Jezreelite had a vineyard; it was in Jezreel next to the palace of King Ahab of Samaria. ² So Ahab spoke to Naboth, saying, "Give me your vineyard so I can have it for a vegetable garden, since it is right next to my palace. I will give you a better vineyard in its place, or if you prefer, I will give you its value in silver."

³ But Naboth said to Ahab, "I will never give my fathers' inheritance to you."

⁴ So Ahab went to his palace resentful and angry because of what Naboth the Jezreelite had told him. He had said, "I will not give you my fathers' inheritance." He lay down on his bed, turned his face away, and didn't eat any food.

⁵ Then his wife Jezebel came to him and said to him, "Why are you so upset that you refuse to eat?"

⁶ "Because I spoke to Naboth the Jezreelite," he replied. "I told him: Give me your vineyard for silver, or if you wish, I will give you a vineyard in its place. But he said, 'I won't give you my vineyard!'"

⁷ Then his wife Jezebel said to him, "Now, exercise your royal power over Israel. Get up, eat some food, and be happy. For I will give you the vineyard of Naboth the Jezreelite." ⁸ So she wrote letters in Ahab's name and sealed them with his seal. She sent the letters to the elders and nobles who lived with Naboth in his city. ⁹ In the letters, she wrote:

Proclaim a fast and seat Naboth at the head of the people. ¹⁰ Then seat two wicked men opposite him and have them testify against him, saying, "You have cursed God and the king!" Then take him out and stone him to death.

¹¹ The men of his city, the elders and nobles who lived in his city, did as Jezebel had sent word to them, just as it was written in the letters she had sent them. ¹² They proclaimed a fast and seated Naboth at the head of the people. ¹³ The two wicked men came in and sat opposite him. Then the wicked men testified against Naboth in the presence of the people, saying, "Naboth has cursed God and the king!" So they took him outside the city and stoned him to death with stones. ¹⁴ Then they sent word to Jezebel: "Naboth has been stoned to death."

¹⁵ When Jezebel heard that Naboth had been stoned to death, she said to Ahab, "Get up and take possession of the vineyard of Naboth the Jezreelite who refused to give it to you for silver, since Naboth isn't alive, but dead." ¹⁶ When Ahab heard that Naboth was dead, he got up to go down to the vineyard of Naboth the Jezreelite to take possession of it.

Still, there was no one like Ahab, who devoted himself to do what was evil in the LORD's sight, because his wife Jezebel incited him.

THE LORD'S JUDGMENT ON AHAB

¹⁷ Then the word of the LORD came to Elijah the Tishbite: ¹⁸ "Get up and go to meet King Ahab of Israel, who is in Samaria. He's in Naboth's vineyard, where he has gone to take possession of it. ¹⁹ Tell him, 'This is what the LORD says: Have you murdered and also taken possession?' Then tell him, 'This is what the LORD says: In the place where the dogs licked up Naboth's blood, the dogs will also lick up your blood!'"

²⁰ Ahab said to Elijah, "So, my enemy, you've found me, have you?"

He replied, "I have found you because you devoted yourself to do what is evil in the LORD's sight. ²¹ This is what the LORD says: 'I am about to bring disaster on you and will eradicate your descendants:

I will wipe out all of Ahab's males,
both slave and free, in Israel;

²² I will make your house like the house of Jeroboam son of Nebat and like the house of Baasha son of Ahijah, because you have angered me and caused Israel to sin.' ²³ The LORD also speaks of Jezebel: 'The dogs will eat Jezebel in the plot of land at Jezreel:

²⁴ Anyone who belongs to Ahab and dies in the city, the dogs will eat,
and anyone who dies in the field, the birds will eat.'"

²⁵ Still, there was no one like Ahab, who devoted himself to do what was evil in the LORD's sight, because his wife Jezebel incited him. ²⁶ He committed the most detestable acts by following idols as the Amorites had, whom the LORD had dispossessed before the Israelites.

²⁷ When Ahab heard these words, he tore his clothes, put sackcloth over his body, and fasted. He lay down in sackcloth and walked around subdued. ²⁸ Then the word of the LORD came to Elijah the Tishbite: ²⁹ "Have you seen how Ahab has humbled himself before me? I will not bring the disaster during his lifetime, because he has humbled himself before me. I will bring the disaster on his house during his son's lifetime."

1 Kings 22

JEHOSHAPHAT'S ALLIANCE WITH AHAB

¹ There was a lull of three years without war between Aram and Israel. ² However, in the third year, King Jehoshaphat of Judah went to visit the king of Israel. ³ The king of Israel had said to his servants, "Don't you know that Ramoth-gilead is ours, but we're doing nothing to take it from the king of Aram?" ⁴ So he asked Jehoshaphat, "Will you go with me to fight Ramoth-gilead?"

Jehoshaphat replied to the king of Israel, "I am as you are, my people as your people, my horses as your horses." ⁵ But Jehoshaphat said to the king of Israel, "First, please ask what the LORD's will is."

⁶ So the king of Israel gathered the prophets, about four hundred men, and asked them, "Should I go against Ramoth-gilead for war or should I refrain?"

They replied, "March up, and the Lord will hand it over to the king."

⁷ But Jehoshaphat asked, "Isn't there a prophet of the LORD here anymore? Let's ask him."

⁸ The king of Israel said to Jehoshaphat, "There is still one man who can inquire of the LORD, but I hate him because he never prophesies good about me, but only disaster. He is Micaiah son of Imlah."

"The king shouldn't say that!" Jehoshaphat replied.

⁹ So the king of Israel called an officer and said, "Hurry and get Micaiah son of Imlah!"

¹⁰ Now the king of Israel and King Jehoshaphat of Judah, clothed in royal attire, were each sitting on his own throne. They were on the threshing floor at the entrance to the gate of Samaria, and all the prophets were prophesying in front of them. ¹¹ Then Zedekiah son of Chenaanah made iron horns and said, "This is what the LORD says: 'You will gore the Arameans with these until they are finished off.'" ¹² And all the prophets were prophesying the same: "March up to Ramoth-gilead and succeed, for the LORD will hand it over to the king."

MICAIAH'S MESSAGE OF DEFEAT

¹³ The messenger who went to call Micaiah instructed him, "Look, the words of the prophets are unanimously favorable for the king. So let your words be like theirs, and speak favorably."

¹⁴ But Micaiah said, "As the LORD lives, I will say whatever the LORD says to me."

¹⁵ So he went to the king, and the king asked him, "Micaiah, should we go to Ramoth-gilead for war, or should we refrain?"

Micaiah told him, "March up and succeed. The LORD will hand it over to the king."

¹⁶ But the king said to him, "How many times must I make you swear not to tell me anything but the truth in the name of the LORD?"

¹⁷ So Micaiah said:

I saw all Israel scattered on the hills
like sheep without a shepherd.
And the LORD said,
"They have no master;
let everyone return home in peace."

¹⁸ So the king of Israel said to Jehoshaphat, "Didn't I tell you he never prophesies good about me, but only disaster?"

¹⁹ Then Micaiah said, "Therefore, hear the word of the LORD: I saw the LORD sitting on his throne, and the whole heavenly army was standing by him at his right hand and at his left hand. ²⁰ And the LORD said, 'Who will entice Ahab to march up and fall at Ramoth-gilead?' So one was saying this and another was saying that.

²¹ "Then a spirit came forward, stood in the LORD's presence, and said, 'I will entice him.'

²² "The LORD asked him, 'How?'

"He said, 'I will go and become a lying spirit in the mouth of all his prophets.'

"Then he said, 'You will certainly entice him and prevail. Go and do that.'

²³ "You see, the LORD has put a lying spirit into the mouth of all these prophets of yours, and the LORD has pronounced disaster against you."

²⁴ Then Zedekiah son of Chenaanah came up, hit Micaiah on the cheek, and demanded, "Did the Spirit of the LORD leave me to speak to you?"

²⁵ Micaiah replied, "You will soon see when you go to hide in an inner chamber on that day."

²⁶ Then the king of Israel ordered, "Take Micaiah and return him to Amon, the governor of the city, and to Joash, the king's son, ²⁷ and say, 'This is what the king says: Put this guy in prison and feed him only a little bread and water until I come back safely.'"

²⁸ But Micaiah said, "If you ever return safely, the LORD has not spoken through me." Then he said, "Listen, all you people!"

AHAB'S DEATH

²⁹ Then the king of Israel and Judah's King Jehoshaphat went up to Ramoth-gilead. ³⁰ But the king of Israel said to Jehoshaphat, "I will disguise myself and go into battle, but you wear your royal attire." So the king of Israel disguised himself and went into battle.

³¹ Now the king of Aram had ordered his thirty-two chariot commanders, "Do not fight with anyone at all except the king of Israel."

³² When the chariot commanders saw Jehoshaphat, they shouted, "He must be the king of Israel!" So they turned to fight against him, but Jehoshaphat cried out. ³³ When the chariot commanders saw that he was not the king of Israel, they turned back from pursuing him.

³⁴ But a man drew his bow without taking special aim and struck the king of Israel through the joints of his armor. So he said to his charioteer, "Turn around and take me out of the battle, for I am badly wounded!" ³⁵ The battle raged throughout that day, and the king was propped up in his chariot facing the Arameans. He died that evening, and blood from his wound flowed into the bottom of the chariot. ³⁶ Then the cry rang out in the army as the sun set, declaring:

Each man to his own city,
and each man to his own land!

³⁷ So the king died and was brought to Samaria. They buried the king in Samaria. ³⁸ Then someone washed the chariot at the pool of Samaria. The dogs licked up his blood, and the prostitutes bathed in it, according to the word of the LORD that he had spoken.

³⁹ The rest of the events of Ahab's reign, along with all his accomplishments, including the ivory palace he built, and all the cities he built, are written in the Historical Record of Israel's Kings. ⁴⁰ Ahab rested with his fathers, and his son Ahaziah became king in his place.

JUDAH'S KING JEHOSHAPHAT

⁴¹ Jehoshaphat son of Asa became king over Judah in the fourth year of Israel's King Ahab. ⁴² Jehoshaphat was thirty-five years old when he became king; he reigned twenty-five years in Jerusalem. His mother's name was Azubah daughter of Shilhi. ⁴³ He walked in all the ways of his father Asa; he did not turn away from them but did what was right in the Lord's sight. However, the high places were not taken away; the people still sacrificed and burned incense on the high places. ⁴⁴ Jehoshaphat also made peace with the king of Israel.

⁴⁵ The rest of the events of Jehoshaphat's reign, along with the might he exercised and how he waged war, are written in the Historical Record of Judah's Kings. ⁴⁶ He eradicated from the land the rest of the male cult prostitutes who were left from the days of his father Asa. ⁴⁷ There was no king in Edom; a deputy served as king. ⁴⁸ Jehoshaphat made ships of Tarshish to go to Ophir for gold, but they did not go because the ships were wrecked at Ezion-geber. ⁴⁹ At that time, Ahaziah son of Ahab said to Jehoshaphat, "Let my servants go with your servants in the ships," but Jehoshaphat was not willing. ⁵⁰ Jehoshaphat rested with his fathers and was buried with them in the city of his ancestor David. His son Jehoram became king in his place.

ISRAEL'S KING AHAZIAH

⁵¹ Ahaziah son of Ahab became king over Israel in Samaria in the seventeenth year of Judah's King Jehoshaphat, and he reigned over Israel two years. ⁵² He did what was evil in the Lord's sight. He walked in the ways of his father, in the ways of his mother, and in the ways of Jeroboam son of Nebat, who had caused Israel to sin. ⁵³ He served Baal and bowed in worship to him. He angered the Lord God of Israel just as his father had done.

Psalm 103:20-22

²⁰ Bless the Lord,
all his angels of great strength,
who do his word,
obedient to his command.
²¹ Bless the Lord, all his armies,
his servants who do his will.
²² Bless the Lord, all his works
in all the places where he rules.
My soul, bless the Lord!

NOTES

As the LORD lives, I will say whatever the LORD says to me.

1 KINGS 22:14

2 KINGS

*For the sake of his servant David, the LORD
was unwilling to destroy Judah…*

2 KINGS 8:19

The Divided Kingdom
From Israel's Ahaziah to the Fall of Israel
2KG 1–17

.
.
.

Ahaziah and the prophet Elijah
1:1–18

Elijah succeeded by Elisha
2:1–25

Israel's King Joram
3:1–27

Elisha's ministry of miracles
4:1–8:15

Judah's King Joram
8:16–24

Judah's King Ahaziah
8:25–29

Israel's King Jehu and the prophet Elisha
9:1–10:36

Queen Athaliah
11:1–16

Three good kings: Joash, Amaziah, Azariah
11:17–15:7

Five bad kings: Zechariah, Shallum, Menahem, Pekahiah, Pekah
15:8–31

Jotham
15:32–38

Ahaz
16:1–20

Hoshea and God's indictment against Israel
17:1–41

The Kingdom of Judah
From King Hezekiah to the Captivity
2KG 18–25

.
.
.

Revival under Hezekiah and apostasy
18:1–21:26

Revival under Josiah and apostasy
22:1–25:7

Jerusalem falls to the Babylonians
25:8–30

Elijah in the Whirlwind

AHAZIAH'S SICKNESS AND DEATH

¹ After Ahab's death, Moab rebelled against Israel. ² Ahaziah had fallen through the latticed window of his upstairs room in Samaria and was injured. So he sent messengers, instructing them, "Go inquire of Baal-zebub, the god of Ekron, whether I will recover from this injury."

³ But the angel of the LORD said to Elijah the Tishbite, "Go and meet the messengers of the king of Samaria and say to them, 'Is it because there is no God in Israel that you are going to inquire of Baal-zebub, the god of Ekron? ⁴ Therefore, this is what the LORD says: You will not get up from your sickbed; you will certainly die.'" Then Elijah left.

⁵ The messengers returned to the king, who asked them, "Why have you come back?"

⁶ They replied, "A man came to meet us and said, 'Go back to the king who sent you and declare to him: This is what the LORD says: Is it because there is no God in Israel that you're sending these men to inquire of Baal-zebub, the god of Ekron? Therefore, you will not get up from your sickbed; you will certainly die.'"

⁷ The king asked them, "What sort of man came up to meet you and spoke those words to you?"

⁸ They replied, "A hairy man with a leather belt around his waist."

He said, "It's Elijah the Tishbite."

⁹ So King Ahaziah sent a captain with his fifty men to Elijah. When the captain went up to him, he was sitting on top of the hill. He announced, "Man of God, the king declares, 'Come down!'"

¹⁰ Elijah responded to the captain, "If I am a man of God, may fire come down from heaven and consume you and your fifty men." Then fire came down from heaven and consumed him and his fifty men.

¹¹ So the king sent another captain with his fifty men to Elijah. He took in the situation and announced, "Man of God, this is what the king says: 'Come down immediately!'"

¹² Elijah responded, "If I am a man of God, may fire come down from heaven and consume you and your fifty men." So a divine fire came down from heaven and consumed him and his fifty men.

¹³ Then the king sent a third captain with his fifty men. The third captain went up and fell on his knees in front of Elijah and begged him, "Man of God, please let my life and the lives of these fifty servants of yours be precious to you. ¹⁴ Already fire has come down from heaven and consumed the first two captains with their companies, but this time let my life be precious to you."

¹⁵ The angel of the LORD said to Elijah, "Go down with him. Don't be afraid of him." So he got up and went down with him to the king.

¹⁶ Then Elijah said to King Ahaziah, "This is what the LORD says: 'Because you have sent messengers to inquire of Baal-zebub, the god of Ekron—is it because there is no God in Israel for you to inquire of his will?—you will not get up from your sickbed; you will certainly die.'"

¹⁷ Ahaziah died according to the word of the LORD that Elijah had spoken. Since he had no son, Joram became king in his place. This happened in the second year of Judah's King Jehoram son of Jehoshaphat. ¹⁸ The rest of the events of Ahaziah's reign, along with his accomplishments, are written in the Historical Record of Israel's Kings.

2 Kings 2

ELIJAH IN THE WHIRLWIND

¹ The time had come for the LORD to take Elijah up to heaven in a whirlwind. Elijah and Elisha were traveling from Gilgal, ² and Elijah said to Elisha, "Stay here; the LORD is sending me on to Bethel."

But Elisha replied, "As the LORD lives and as you yourself live, I will not leave you." So they went down to Bethel.

³ Then the sons of the prophets who were at Bethel came out to Elisha and said, "Do you know that the LORD will take your master away from you today?"

He said, "Yes, I know. Be quiet."

⁴ Elijah said to him, "Elisha, stay here; the LORD is sending me to Jericho."

But Elisha said, "As the LORD lives and as you yourself live, I will not leave you." So they went to Jericho.

⁵ Then the sons of the prophets who were in Jericho came up to Elisha and said, "Do you know that the LORD will take your master away from you today?"

He said, "Yes, I know. Be quiet."

⁶ Elijah said to him, "Stay here; the LORD is sending me to the Jordan."

But Elisha said, "As the LORD lives and as you yourself live, I will not leave you." So the two of them went on.

⁷ Fifty men from the sons of the prophets came and stood observing them at a distance while the two of them stood by the Jordan. ⁸ Elijah took his mantle, rolled it up, and struck the water, which parted to the right and left. Then the two of them crossed over on dry ground. ⁹ When they had crossed over, Elijah said to Elisha, "Tell me what I can do for you before I am taken from you."

So Elisha answered, "Please, let me inherit two shares of your spirit."

¹⁰ Elijah replied, "You have asked for something difficult. If you see me being taken from you, you will have it. If not, you won't."

¹¹ As they continued walking and talking, a chariot of fire with horses of fire suddenly appeared and separated the two of them. Then Elijah went up into heaven in the whirlwind. ¹² As Elisha watched, he kept crying out, "My father, my father, the chariots and horsemen of Israel!"

ELISHA SUCCEEDS ELIJAH

When he could see him no longer, he took hold of his own clothes, tore them in two, ¹³ picked up the mantle that had fallen off Elijah, and went back and stood on the bank of the Jordan. [14] He took the mantle Elijah had dropped, and he struck the water. "Where is the LORD God of Elijah?" he asked. He struck the water himself, and it parted to the right and the left, and Elisha crossed over.

[15] When the sons of the prophets from Jericho who were observing saw him, they said, "The spirit of Elijah rests on Elisha." They came to meet him and bowed down to the ground in front of him.

[16] Then the sons of the prophets said to Elisha, "Since there are fifty strong men here with your servants, please let them go and search for your master. Maybe the Spirit of the LORD has carried him away and put him on one of the mountains or into one of the valleys."

He answered, "Don't send them."

[17] However, they urged him to the point of embarrassment, so he said, "Send them." They sent fifty men, who looked for three days but did not find him. [18] When they returned to him in Jericho where he was staying, he said to them, "Didn't I tell you not to go?"

[19] The men of the city said to Elisha, "My lord can see that even though the city's location is good, the water is bad and the land unfruitful."

[20] He replied, "Bring me a new bowl and put salt in it."

After they had brought him one, [21] Elisha went out to the spring, threw salt in it, and said, "This is what the LORD says: 'I have healed this water. No longer will death or unfruit-fulness result from it.'" [22] Therefore, the water still remains healthy today according to the word that Elisha spoke.

[23] From there Elisha went up to Bethel. As he was walking up the path, some small boys came out of the city and jeered at him, chanting, "Go up, baldy! Go up, baldy!" [24] He turned around, looked at them, and cursed them in the name of the LORD. Then two female bears came out of the woods and mauled forty-two of the children. [25] From there Elisha went to Mount Carmel, and then he returned to Samaria.

Romans 11:1–6

ISRAEL'S REJECTION NOT TOTAL

[1] I ask, then, has God rejected his people? Absolutely not! For I too am an Israelite, a descendant of Abraham, from the tribe of Benjamin. [2] God has not rejected his people whom he foreknew. Or don't you know what the Scripture says in the passage about Elijah—how he pleads with God against Israel? [3] Lord, they have killed your prophets and torn down your altars. I am the only one left, and they are trying to take my life! [4] But what was God's answer to him? I have left seven thousand for myself who have not bowed down to Baal. [5] In the same way, then, there is also at the present time a remnant chosen by grace. [6] Now if by grace, then it is not by works; otherwise grace ceases to be grace.

NOTES

As the Lord lives and as you yourself live, I will not leave you.

2 KINGS 2:4

Grace Day

Use this day to pray, rest, and reflect on this week's
reading, giving thanks for the grace that is ours in Christ.

Bless the Lord, all his works
in all the places where he rules.
My soul, bless the Lord!

PSALM 103:22

DATE

WEEKLY

DAY · · · 14

TRUTH

Scripture is God-breathed and true. When we memorize it, we carry the gospel with us wherever we go.

This week we will memorize the key verse for 1 Kings, a statement of God's power over all others.

Find the corresponding memory card in the back of this book.

When all the people saw it, they fell facedown and said, "The LORD, he is God! The LORD, he is God!"

. . .

1 KINGS 18:39

Elisha's Ministry

2 Kings 3

ISRAEL'S KING JORAM

¹ Joram son of Ahab became king over Israel in Samaria during the eighteenth year of Judah's King Jehoshaphat, and he reigned twelve years. ² He did what was evil in the LORD's sight, but not like his father and mother, for he removed the sacred pillar of Baal his father had made. ³ Nevertheless, Joram clung to the sins that Jeroboam son of Nebat had caused Israel to commit. He did not turn away from them.

MOAB'S REBELLION AGAINST ISRAEL

⁴ King Mesha of Moab was a sheep breeder. He used to pay the king of Israel one hundred thousand lambs and the wool of one hundred thousand rams, ⁵ but when Ahab died, the king of Moab rebelled against the king of Israel. ⁶ So King Joram marched out from Samaria at that time and mobilized all Israel. ⁷ Then he sent a message to King Jehoshaphat of Judah: "The king of Moab has rebelled against me. Will you go with me to fight against Moab?"

Jehoshaphat said, "I will go. I am as you are, my people as your people, my horses as your horses."

⁸ He asked, "Which route should we take?"

He replied, "The route of the Wilderness of Edom."

⁹ So the king of Israel, the king of Judah, and the king of Edom set out. After they had traveled their indirect route for seven days, they had no water for the army or the animals with them.

¹⁰ Then the king of Israel said, "Oh no, the LORD has summoned these three kings, only to hand them over to Moab."

¹¹ But Jehoshaphat said, "Isn't there a prophet of the LORD here? Let's inquire of the LORD through him."

One of the servants of the king of Israel answered, "Elisha son of Shaphat, who used to pour water on Elijah's hands, is here."

¹² Jehoshaphat affirmed, "The word of the LORD is with him." So the king of Israel and Jehoshaphat and the king of Edom went to him.

¹³ However, Elisha said to King Joram of Israel, "What do we have in common? Go to the prophets of your father and your mother!"

But the king of Israel replied, "No, because it is the LORD who has summoned these three kings to hand them over to Moab."

14 Elisha responded, "By the life of the LORD of Armies, before whom I stand: If I did not have respect for King Jehoshaphat of Judah, I wouldn't look at you; I would not take notice of you. 15 Now, bring me a musician."

While the musician played, the LORD's hand came on Elisha. 16 Then he said, "This is what the LORD says: 'Dig ditch after ditch in this wadi.' 17 For the LORD says, 'You will not see wind or rain, but the wadi will be filled with water, and you will drink—you and your cattle and your animals.' 18 This is easy in the LORD's sight. He will also hand Moab over to you. 19 Then you will attack every fortified city and every choice city. You will cut down every good tree and stop up every spring. You will ruin every good piece of land with stones."

20 About the time for the grain offering the next morning, water suddenly came from the direction of Edom and filled the land.

21 All Moab had heard that the kings had come up to fight against them. So all who could bear arms, from the youngest to the oldest, were summoned and took their stand at the border. 22 When they got up early in the morning, the sun was shining on the water, and the Moabites saw that the water across from them was red like blood. 23 "This is blood!" they exclaimed. "The kings have crossed swords and their men have killed one another. So, to the spoil, Moab!"

24 However, when the Moabites came to Israel's camp, the Israelites attacked them, and they fled from them. So Israel went into the land attacking the Moabites. 25 They would destroy the cities, and each of them would throw a stone to cover every good piece of land. They would stop up every spring and cut down every good tree. This went on until only the buildings of Kir-hareseth were left. Then men with slings surrounded the city and attacked it.

26 When the king of Moab saw that the battle was too fierce for him, he took seven hundred swordsmen with him to try to break through to the king of Edom, but they could not do it. 27 So he took his firstborn son, who was to become king in his place, and offered him as a burnt offering on the city wall. Great wrath was on the Israelites, and they withdrew from him and returned to their land.

2 Kings 4

THE WIDOW'S OIL MULTIPLIED

1 One of the wives of the sons of the prophets cried out to Elisha, "Your servant, my husband, has died. You know that your servant feared the LORD. Now the creditor is coming to take my two children as his slaves."

2 Elisha asked her, "What can I do for you? Tell me, what do you have in the house?"

She said, "Your servant has nothing in the house except a jar of oil."

3 Then he said, "Go out and borrow empty containers from all your neighbors. Do not get just a few. 4 Then go in and shut the door behind you and your sons, and pour oil into all these containers. Set the full ones to one side." 5 So she left.

After she had shut the door behind her and her sons, they kept bringing her containers, and she kept pouring. 6 When they were full, she said to her son, "Bring me another container."

But he replied, "There aren't any more." Then the oil stopped.

7 She went and told the man of God, and he said, "Go sell the oil and pay your debt; you and your sons can live on the rest."

THE SHUNAMMITE WOMAN'S HOSPITALITY

8 One day Elisha went to Shunem. A prominent woman who lived there persuaded him to eat some food. So whenever he passed by, he stopped there to eat. 9 Then she said to her husband, "I know that the one who often passes by here is a holy man of God, 10 so let's make a small, walled-in upper room and put a bed, a table, a chair, and a lamp there for him. Whenever he comes, he can stay there."

"As the Lord lives and as you yourself live, I will not leave you."

2 KINGS 4:30

THE SHUNAMMITE WOMAN'S SON

¹¹ One day he came there and stopped at the upstairs room to lie down. ¹² He ordered his attendant Gehazi, "Call this Shunammite woman." So he called her and she stood before him.

¹³ Then he said to Gehazi, "Say to her, 'Look, you've gone to all this trouble for us. What can we do for you? Can we speak on your behalf to the king or to the commander of the army?'"

She answered, "I am living among my own people."

¹⁴ So he asked, "Then what should be done for her?"

Gehazi answered, "Well, she has no son, and her husband is old."

¹⁵ "Call her," Elisha said. So Gehazi called her, and she stood in the doorway. ¹⁶ Elisha said, "At this time next year you will have a son in your arms."

Then she said, "No, my lord. Man of God, do not lie to your servant."

¹⁷ The woman conceived and gave birth to a son at the same time the following year, as Elisha had promised her.

THE SHUNAMMITE'S SON RAISED

¹⁸ The child grew and one day went out to his father and the harvesters. ¹⁹ Suddenly he complained to his father, "My head! My head!"

His father told his servant, "Carry him to his mother." ²⁰ So he picked him up and took him to his mother. The child sat on her lap until noon and then died. ²¹ She went up and laid him on the bed of the man of God, shut him in, and left.

²² She summoned her husband and said, "Please send me one of the servants and one of the donkeys, so I can hurry to the man of God and come back again."

²³ But he said, "Why go to him today? It's not a New Moon or a Sabbath."

She replied, "Everything is all right."

²⁴ Then she saddled the donkey and said to her servant, "Go fast; don't slow the pace for me unless I tell you." ²⁵ So she came to the man of God at Mount Carmel.

When the man of God saw her at a distance, he said to his attendant Gehazi, "Look, there's the Shunammite woman. ²⁶ Run out to meet her and ask, 'Are you all right? Is your husband all right? Is your son all right?'"

And she answered, "Everything's all right."

27 When she came up to the man of God at the mountain, she clung to his feet. Gehazi came to push her away, but the man of God said, "Leave her alone—she is in severe anguish, and the LORD has hidden it from me. He hasn't told me."

28 Then she said, "Did I ask my lord for a son? Didn't I say, 'Do not lie to me?'"

29 So Elisha said to Gehazi, "Tuck your mantle under your belt, take my staff with you, and go. If you meet anyone, don't stop to greet him, and if a man greets you, don't answer him. Then place my staff on the boy's face."

30 The boy's mother said to Elisha, "As the LORD lives and as you yourself live, I will not leave you." So he got up and followed her.

31 Gehazi went ahead of them and placed the staff on the boy's face, but there was no sound or sign of life, so he went back to meet Elisha and told him, "The boy didn't wake up."

32 When Elisha got to the house, he discovered the boy lying dead on his bed. 33 So he went in, closed the door behind the two of them, and prayed to the LORD. 34 Then he went up and lay on the boy: he put mouth to mouth, eye to eye, hand to hand. While he bent down over him, the boy's flesh became warm. 35 Elisha got up, went into the house, and paced back and forth. Then he went up and bent down over him again. The boy sneezed seven times and opened his eyes.

36 Elisha called Gehazi and said, "Call the Shunammite woman." He called her and she came. Then Elisha said, "Pick up your son." 37 She came, fell at his feet, and bowed to the ground; she picked up her son and left.

THE DEADLY STEW

38 When Elisha returned to Gilgal, there was a famine in the land. The sons of the prophets were sitting before him. He said to his attendant, "Put on the large pot and make stew for the sons of the prophets."

39 One went out to the field to gather herbs and found a wild vine from which he gathered as many wild gourds as his garment would hold. Then he came back and cut them up into the pot of stew, but they were unaware of what they were.

40 They served some for the men to eat, but when they ate the stew they cried out, "There's death in the pot, man of God!" And they were unable to eat it.

41 Then Elisha said, "Get some flour." He threw it into the pot and said, "Serve it for the people to eat." And there was nothing bad in the pot.

THE MULTIPLIED BREAD

42 A man from Baal-shalishah came to the man of God with his sack full of twenty loaves of barley bread from the first bread of the harvest. Elisha said, "Give it to the people to eat."

43 But Elisha's attendant asked, "What? Am I to set this before a hundred men?"

"Give it to the people to eat," Elisha said, "for this is what the LORD says: 'They will eat, and they will have some left over.'" 44 So he set it before them, and as the LORD had promised, they ate and had some left over.

2 Kings 5

NAAMAN'S DISEASE HEALED

1 **Naaman**, commander of the army for the king of Aram, was a man important to his master and highly regarded because through him, the LORD had given victory to Aram. The man was a valiant warrior, but he had a skin disease.

2 Aram had gone on raids and brought back from the land of Israel a young girl who served Naaman's wife. 3 She said to her mistress, "If only my master were with the prophet who is in Samaria, he would cure him of his skin disease."

4 So Naaman went and told his master what the girl from the land of Israel had said. 5 Therefore, the king of Aram said, "Go, and I will send a letter with you to the king of Israel."

So he went and took with him 750 pounds of silver, 150 pounds of gold, and ten sets of clothing. ⁶ He brought the letter to the king of Israel, and it read:

> When this letter comes to you, note that I have sent you my servant Naaman for you to cure him of his skin disease.

⁷ When the king of Israel read the letter, he tore his clothes and asked, "Am I God, killing and giving life that this man expects me to cure a man of his skin disease? Recognize that he is only picking a fight with me."

⁸ When Elisha the man of God heard that the king of Israel had torn his clothes, he sent a message to the king, "Why have you torn your clothes? Have him come to me, and he will know there is a prophet in Israel." ⁹ So Naaman came with his horses and chariots and stood at the door of Elisha's house.

¹⁰ Then Elisha sent him a messenger, who said, "Go wash seven times in the Jordan and your skin will be restored and you will be clean."

¹¹ But Naaman got angry and left, saying, "I was telling myself: He will surely come out, stand and call on the name of the LORD his God, and wave his hand over the place and cure the skin disease. ¹² Aren't Abana and Pharpar, the rivers of Damascus, better than all the waters of Israel? Couldn't I wash in them and be clean?" So he turned and left in a rage.

¹³ But his servants approached and said to him, "My father, if the prophet had told you to do some great thing, would you not have done it? How much more should you do it when he only tells you, 'Wash and be clean'?" ¹⁴ So Naaman went down and dipped himself in the Jordan seven times, according to the command of the man of God. Then his skin was restored and became like the skin of a small boy, and he was clean.

¹⁵ Then Naaman and his whole company went back to the man of God, stood before him, and declared, "I know there's no God in the whole world except in Israel. Therefore, please accept a gift from your servant."

¹⁶ But Elisha said, "As the LORD lives, in whose presence I stand, I will not accept it." Naaman urged him to accept it, but he refused.

¹⁷ Naaman responded, "If not, please let your servant be given as much soil as a pair of mules can carry, for your servant will no longer offer a burnt offering or a sacrifice to any other god but the LORD. ¹⁸ However, in a particular matter may the LORD pardon your servant: When my master, the king of Aram, goes into the temple of **Rimmon** to bow in worship while he is leaning on my arm, and I have to bow in the temple of Rimmon—when I bow in the temple of Rimmon, may the LORD pardon your servant in this matter."

¹⁹ So he said to him, "Go in peace."

GEHAZI'S GREED PUNISHED

After Naaman had traveled a short distance from Elisha, ²⁰ Gehazi, the attendant of Elisha the man of God, thought, "My master has let this Aramean Naaman off lightly by not accepting from him what he brought. As the LORD lives, I will run after him and get something from him."

²¹ So Gehazi pursued Naaman. When Naaman saw someone running after him, he got down from the chariot to meet him and asked, "Is everything all right?"

²² Gehazi said, "It's all right. My master has sent me to say, 'I have just now discovered that two young men from the sons of the prophets have come to me from the hill country of Ephraim. Please give them seventy-five pounds of silver and two sets of clothing.'"

²³ But Naaman insisted, "Please, accept one hundred fifty pounds." He urged Gehazi and then packed one hundred fifty pounds of silver in two bags with two sets of clothing. Naaman gave them to two of his attendants who carried them ahead of Gehazi. ²⁴ When Gehazi came to the hill, he took the gifts from them and deposited them in the house. Then he dismissed the men, and they left.

²⁵ Gehazi came and stood by his master. "Where did you go, Gehazi?" Elisha asked him.

He replied, "Your servant didn't go anywhere."

[26] "And my heart didn't go when the man got down from his chariot to meet you," Elisha said. "Is this a time to accept silver and clothing, olive orchards and vineyards, flocks and herds, and male and female slaves? [27] Therefore, Naaman's skin disease will cling to you and your descendants forever." So Gehazi went out from his presence diseased, resembling snow.

John 4:10

Jesus answered, "If you knew the gift of God, and who is saying to you, 'Give me a drink,' you would ask him, and he would give you living water."

ELISHA & JESUS

Though it may not be immediately apparent, there is a strong connection between the ministry of Jesus and the books of 1 and 2 Kings. Specifically, many aspects of Elisha's life and ministry foreshadow the work of Jesus. This chart highlights several parallels between Elisha and Jesus.

ELISHA

ELISHA MEANS "MY GOD SAVES."

1KG 19:19–21

ELIJAH WAS THE FORERUNNER OF ELISHA.

2KG 2:7–15

THE SPIRIT OF ELIJAH RESTED ON ELISHA ON THE FAR SIDE OF THE JORDAN.

2KG 4:1–7

ELISHA RAISED A DEAD SON TO LIFE AND RESTORED HIM TO HIS MOTHER.

2KG 4:34–35

ELISHA HEALED THE SICK.

JESUS

JESUS MEANS "YAHWEH SAVES."

JOHN THE BAPTIST, WHO CAME IN THE SPIRIT AND POWER OF ELIJAH, WAS THE FORERUNNER OF JESUS.

MT 3:1–12; 17:10–13

THE HOLY SPIRIT RESTED ON JESUS ON THE FAR SIDE OF THE JORDAN.

JN 1:28–34

JESUS RAISED A DEAD SON TO LIFE AND RESTORED HIM TO HIS MOTHER.

LK 7:11–17

JESUS HEALED THE SICK.

MT 4:23

2KG 4:42–44

ELISHA
MULTIPLIED
BREAD TO FEED
A CROWD.

2KG 5:1–16

ELISHA
CLEANSED
A LEPER.

2KG 5:1–16

ELISHA
MINISTERED TO A
GENTILE MILITARY
OFFICER.

2KG 5:20–24

ELISHA HAD A
DISCIPLE WHO
WENT BEHIND
HIS BACK FOR
MONEY.

2KG 13:21

A RESURRECTION
TOOK PLACE IN
ELISHA'S TOMB.

JESUS TWICE
MULTIPLIED FISH
AND BREAD TO
FEED A CROWD.

MK 6:30–44;
8:1–10

JESUS CLEANSED
LEPERS.

MK 1:40–45;
LK 17:11–19

JESUS MINISTERED
TO A GENTILE
MILITARY OFFICER.

MT 8:5–13

JESUS HAD A
DISCIPLE WHO
WENT BEHIND
HIS BACK FOR
MONEY.

MK 14:10–11

A RESURRECTION
TOOK PLACE IN
JESUS'S TOMB.

MT 28:5–6

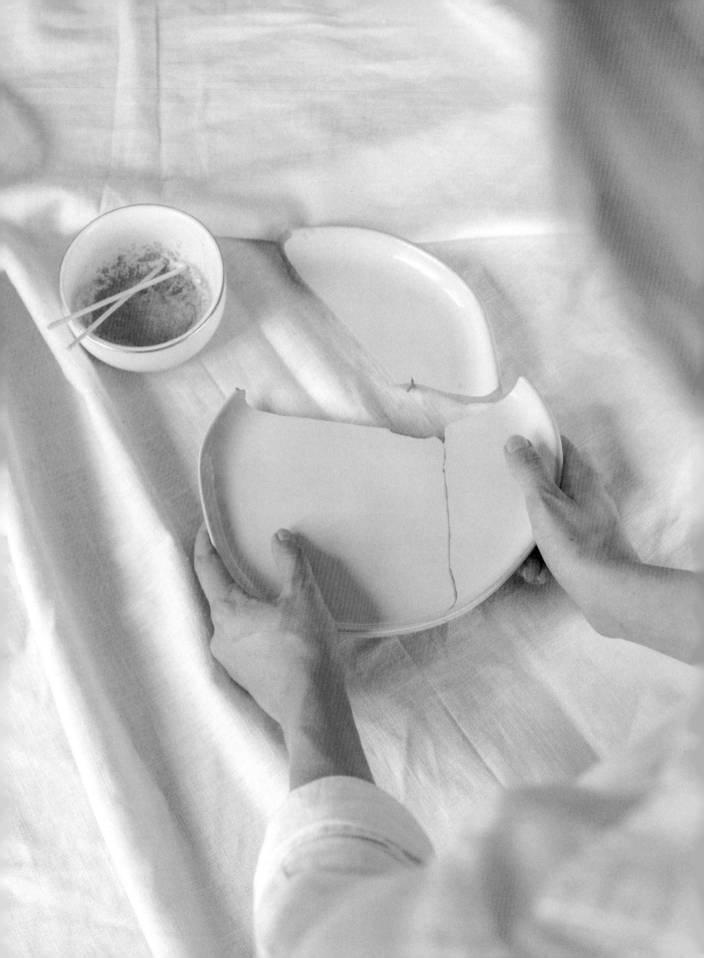

Elisha's Ministry Continues

THE FLOATING AX HEAD

¹ The sons of the prophets said to Elisha, "Please notice that the place where we live under your supervision is too small for us. ² Please let us go to the Jordan where we can each get a log and can build ourselves a place to live there."

"Go," he said.

³ Then one said, "Please come with your servants."

"I'll come," he answered.

⁴ So he went with them, and when they came to the Jordan, they cut down trees. ⁵ As one of them was cutting down a tree, the iron ax head fell into the water, and he cried out, "Oh, my master, it was borrowed!"

⁶ Then the man of God asked, "Where did it fall?"

When he showed him the place, the man of God cut a piece of wood, threw it there, and made the iron float. ⁷ Then he said, "Pick it up." So he reached out and took it.

THE ARAMEAN WAR

⁸ When the king of Aram was waging war against Israel, he conferred with his servants, "My camp will be at such and such a place."

⁹ But the man of God sent word to the king of Israel: "Be careful passing by this place, for the Arameans are going down there." ¹⁰ Consequently, the king of Israel sent word to the place the man of God had told him about. The man of God repeatedly warned the king, so the king would be on his guard.

¹¹ The king of Aram was enraged because of this matter, and he called his servants and demanded of them, "Tell me, which one of us is for the king of Israel?"

¹² One of his servants said, "No one, my lord the king. Elisha, the prophet in Israel, tells the king of Israel even the words you speak in your bedroom."

¹³ So the king said, "Go and see where he is, so I can send men to capture him."

When he was told, "Elisha is in Dothan," ¹⁴ he sent horses, chariots, and a massive army there. They went by night and surrounded the city.

DAY

1
6

Jehoram

Israel

¹⁵ When the servant of the man of God got up early and went out, he discovered an army with horses and chariots surrounding the city. So he asked Elisha, "Oh, my master, what are we to do?"

¹⁶ Elisha said, "Don't be afraid, for those who are with us outnumber those who are with them."

¹⁷ Then Elisha prayed, "LORD, please open his eyes and let him see." So the LORD opened the servant's eyes, and he saw that the mountain was covered with horses and chariots of fire all around Elisha.

¹⁸ When the Arameans came against him, Elisha prayed to the LORD, "Please strike this nation with blindness." So he struck them with blindness, according to Elisha's word. ¹⁹ Then Elisha said to them, "This is not the way, and this is not the city. Follow me, and I will take you to the man you're looking for." And he led them to Samaria. ²⁰ When they entered Samaria, Elisha said, "LORD, open these men's eyes and let them see." So the LORD opened their eyes, and they saw that they were in the middle of Samaria.

²¹ When the king of Israel saw them, he said to Elisha, "Should I kill them, should I kill them, my father?"

²² Elisha replied, "Don't kill them. Do you kill those you have captured with your sword or your bow? Set food and water in front of them so they can eat and drink and go to their master."

²³ So he prepared a big feast for them. When they had eaten and drunk, he sent them away, and they went to their master. The Aramean raiders did not come into Israel's land again.

THE SIEGE OF SAMARIA

²⁴ Some time later, King Ben-hadad of Aram brought all his military units together and marched up and laid siege to Samaria. ²⁵ So there was a severe famine in Samaria, and they continued the siege against it until a donkey's head sold for thirty-four ounces of silver, and a cup of dove's dung sold for two ounces of silver.

²⁶ As the king of Israel was passing by on the wall, a woman cried out to him, "My lord the king, help!"

²⁷ He answered, "If the LORD doesn't help you, where can I get help for you? From the threshing floor or the winepress?" ²⁸ Then the king asked her, "What's the matter?"

She said, "This woman said to me, 'Give up your son, and we will eat him today. Then we will eat my son tomorrow.' ²⁹ So we boiled my son and ate him, and I said to her the next day, 'Give up your son, and we will eat him,' but she has hidden her son."

³⁰ When the king heard the woman's words, he tore his clothes. Then, as he was passing by on the wall, the people saw that there was sackcloth under his clothes next to his skin. ³¹ He announced, "May God punish me and do so severely if the head of Elisha son of Shaphat remains on his shoulders today."

³² Elisha was sitting in his house, and the elders were sitting with him. The king sent a man ahead of him, but before the messenger got to him, Elisha said to the elders, "Do you see how this murderer has sent someone to remove my head? Look, when the messenger comes, shut the door to keep him out. Isn't the sound of his master's feet behind him?"

³³ While Elisha was still speaking with them, the messenger came down to him. Then he said, "This disaster is from the LORD. Why should I wait for the LORD any longer?"

2 Kings 7

¹ Elisha replied, "Hear the word of the LORD! This is what the LORD says: 'About this time tomorrow at Samaria's gate, six quarts of fine flour will sell for a half ounce of silver and twelve quarts of barley will sell for a half ounce of silver.'"

² Then the captain, the king's right-hand man, responded to the man of God, "Look, even if the LORD were to make windows in heaven, could this really happen?"

Elisha announced, "You will in fact see it with your own eyes, but you won't eat any of it."

³ Now four men with a skin disease were at the entrance to the city gate. They said to each other, "Why just sit here until we die? ⁴ If we say, 'Let's go into the city,' we will die there because the famine is in the city, but if we sit here, we will also die. So now, come on. Let's surrender to the Arameans' camp. If they let us live, we will live; if they kill us, we will die."

⁵ So the diseased men got up at twilight to go to the Arameans' camp. When they came to the camp's edge, they discovered that no one was there, ⁶ for the Lord had caused the Aramean camp to hear the sound of chariots, horses, and a large army. The Arameans had said to each other, "The king of Israel must have hired the kings of the Hittites and the kings of Egypt to attack us." ⁷ So they had gotten up and fled at twilight, abandoning their tents, horses, and donkeys. The camp was intact, and they had fled for their lives.

⁸ When these diseased men came to the edge of the camp, they went into a tent to eat and drink. Then they picked up the silver, gold, and clothing and went off and hid them. They came back and entered another tent, picked things up, and hid them. ⁹ Then they said to each other, "We're not doing what is right. Today is a day of good news. If we are silent and wait until morning light, our punishment will catch up with us. So let's go tell the king's household."

¹⁰ The diseased men came and called to the city's gatekeepers and told them, "We went to the Aramean camp and no one was there—no human sounds. There was nothing but tethered horses and donkeys, and the tents were intact." ¹¹ The gatekeepers called out, and the news was reported to the king's household.

¹² So the king got up in the night and said to his servants, "Let me tell you what the Arameans have done to us. They know we are starving, so they have left the camp to hide in the open country, thinking, 'When they come out of the city, we will take them alive and go into the city.'"

¹³ But one of his servants responded, "Please, let messengers take five of the horses that are left in the city. Their fate is like the entire Israelite community who will die, so let's send them and see."

¹⁴ The messengers took two chariots with horses, and the king sent them after the Aramean army, saying, "Go and see." ¹⁵ So they followed them as far as the Jordan. They saw that the whole way was littered with clothes and equipment the Arameans had thrown off in their haste. The messengers returned and told the king.

¹⁶ Then the people went out and plundered the Aramean camp. It was then that six quarts of fine flour sold for a half ounce of silver and twelve quarts of barley sold for a half ounce of silver, according to the word of the LORD. ¹⁷ The king had appointed the captain, his right-hand man, to be in charge of the city gate, but the people trampled him in the gate. He died, just as the man of God had predicted when the king had come to him. ¹⁸ When the man of God had said to the king, "About this time tomorrow twelve quarts of barley will sell for a half ounce of silver and six quarts of fine flour will sell for a half ounce of silver at Samaria's gate," ¹⁹ this captain had answered the man of God, "Look, even if the LORD were to make windows in heaven, could this really happen?" Elisha had said, "You will in fact see it with your own eyes, but you won't eat any of it." ²⁰ This is what happened to him: the people trampled him in the city gate, and he died.

2 Kings 8:1–15

THE SHUNAMMITE'S LAND RESTORED

¹ Elisha said to the woman whose son he had restored to life, "Get ready, you and your household, and go live as a resident alien wherever you can. For the LORD has announced a seven-year famine, and it has already come to the land."

² So the woman got ready and did what the man of God said. She and her household lived as resident aliens in the land of the Philistines for seven years. ³ When the woman returned from the land of the Philistines at the end of seven years, she went to appeal to the king for her house and field.

⁴ The king had been speaking to Gehazi, the attendant of the man of God, saying, "Tell me all the great things Elisha has done."

⁵ While he was telling the king how Elisha restored the dead son to life, the woman whose son he had restored to life came to appeal to the king for her house and field. So Gehazi said, "My lord the king, this is the woman and this is the son Elisha restored to life."

⁶ When the king asked the woman, she told him the story. So the king appointed a court official for her, saying, "Restore all that was hers, along with all the income from the field from the day she left the country until now."

ARAM'S KING HAZAEL

⁷ Elisha came to Damascus while King Ben-hadad of Aram was sick, and the king was told, "The man of God has come here." ⁸ So the king said to Hazael, "Take a gift with you and go meet the man of God. Inquire of the LORD through him, 'Will I recover from this sickness?'"

⁹ Hazael went to meet Elisha, taking with him a gift: forty camel-loads of all the finest products of Damascus. When he came and stood before him, he said, "Your son, King Ben-hadad of Aram, has sent me to ask you, 'Will I recover from this sickness?'"

¹⁰ Elisha told him, "Go say to him, 'You are sure to recover.' But the LORD has shown me that he is sure to die." ¹¹ Then he stared steadily at him until he was ashamed.

The man of God wept, ¹² and Hazael asked, "Why is my lord weeping?"

He replied, "Because I know the evil you will do to the people of Israel. You will set their fortresses on fire. You will kill their young men with the sword. You will dash their children to pieces. You will rip open their pregnant women."

¹³ Hazael said, "How could your servant, a mere dog, do such a mighty deed?"

Elisha answered, "The LORD has shown me that you will be king over Aram."

¹⁴ Hazael left Elisha and went to his master, who asked him, "What did Elisha say to you?"

He responded, "He told me you are sure to recover." ¹⁵ The next day Hazael took a heavy cloth, dipped it in water, and spread it over the king's face. Ben-hadad died, and Hazael reigned in his place.

Deuteronomy 6:10–12

REMEMBERING GOD THROUGH OBEDIENCE

¹⁰ When the LORD your God brings you into the land he swore to your fathers Abraham, Isaac, and Jacob that he would give you—a land with large and beautiful cities that you did not build, ¹¹ houses full of every good thing that you did not fill them with, cisterns that you did not dig, and vineyards and olive groves that you did not plant—and when you eat and are satisfied, ¹² be careful not to forget the LORD who brought you out of the land of Egypt, out of the place of slavery.

NOTES

Lord, please open his eyes and let him see.

Attempts at Reform

DAY

1
7

Jehoram, Ahaziah, Jehu

Judah, Israel

2 Kings 8:16–29

JUDAH'S KING JEHORAM

16 In the fifth year of Israel's King Joram son of Ahab, Jehoram son of Jehoshaphat became king of Judah, replacing his father. 17 He was thirty-two years old when he became king, and he reigned eight years in Jerusalem. 18 He walked in the ways of the kings of Israel, as the house of Ahab had done, for Ahab's daughter was his wife. He did what was evil in the Lord's sight. 19 For the sake of his servant David, the Lord was unwilling to destroy Judah, since he had promised to give a lamp to David and his sons forever.

20 During Jehoram's reign, Edom rebelled against Judah's control and appointed their own king. 21 So Jehoram crossed over to Zair with all his chariots. Then at night he set out to attack the Edomites who had surrounded him and the chariot commanders, but his troops fled to their tents. 22 So Edom is still in rebellion against Judah's control today. Libnah also rebelled at that time.

23 The rest of the events of Jehoram's reign, along with all his accomplishments, are written in the Historical Record of Judah's Kings. 24 Jehoram rested with his fathers and was buried with his fathers in the city of David, and his son Ahaziah became king in his place.

JUDAH'S KING AHAZIAH

25 In the twelfth year of Israel's King Joram son of Ahab, Ahaziah son of Jehoram became king of Judah. 26 Ahaziah was twenty-two years old when he became king, and he reigned one year in Jerusalem. His mother's name was Athaliah, granddaughter of Israel's King Omri. 27 He walked in the ways of the house of Ahab and did what was evil in the Lord's sight like the house of Ahab, for his father had married into the house of Ahab.

28 Ahaziah went with Joram son of Ahab to fight against King Hazael of Aram in Ramoth-gilead, and the Arameans wounded Joram. 29 So King Joram returned to Jezreel to recover from the wounds that the Arameans had inflicted on him in Ramoth-gilead when he fought against Aram's King Hazael. Then Judah's King Ahaziah son of Jehoram went down to Jezreel to visit Joram son of Ahab since Joram was ill.

2 Kings 9

JEHU ANOINTED AS ISRAEL'S KING

1 The prophet Elisha called one of the sons of the prophets and said, "Tuck your mantle under your belt, take this flask of oil with you, and go to Ramoth-gilead. 2 When you get there, look for Jehu son of Jehoshaphat,

son of Nimshi. Go in, get him away from his colleagues, and take him to an inner room. ³ Then take the flask of oil, pour it on his head, and say, 'This is what the LORD says: "I anoint you king over Israel."' Open the door and escape. Don't wait." ⁴ So the young prophet went to Ramoth-gilead.

⁵ When he arrived, the army commanders were sitting there, so he said, "I have a message for you, commander."

Jehu asked, "For which one of us?"

He answered, "For you, commander."

⁶ So Jehu got up and went into the house. The young prophet poured the oil on his head and said, "This is what the LORD God of Israel says: 'I anoint you king over the LORD's people, Israel. ⁷ You are to strike down the house of your master Ahab so that I may avenge the blood shed by the hand of Jezebel—the blood of my servants the prophets and of all the servants of the LORD. ⁸ The whole house of Ahab will perish, and I will wipe out all of Ahab's males, both slave and free, in Israel. ⁹ I will make the house of Ahab like the house of Jeroboam son of Nebat and like the house of Baasha son of Ahijah. ¹⁰ The dogs will eat Jezebel in the plot of land at Jezreel—no one will bury her.'" Then the young prophet opened the door and escaped.

¹¹ When Jehu came out to his master's servants, they asked, "Is everything all right? Why did this crazy person come to you?"

Then he said to them, "You know the sort and their ranting."

¹² But they replied, "That's a lie! Tell us!"

So Jehu said, "He talked to me about this and that and said, 'This is what the LORD says: I anoint you king over Israel.'"

¹³ Each man quickly took his garment and put it under Jehu on the bare steps. They blew the ram's horn and proclaimed, "Jehu is king!"

¹⁴ Then Jehu son of Jehoshaphat, son of Nimshi, conspired against Joram. Joram and all Israel had been at Ramoth-gilead on guard against King Hazael of Aram. ¹⁵ But King Joram had returned to Jezreel to recover from the wounds that the Arameans had inflicted on him when he fought against Aram's King Hazael. Jehu said, "If you commanders wish to make me king, then don't let anyone escape from the city to go tell about it in Jezreel."

JEHU KILLS JORAM AND AHAZIAH

¹⁶ Jehu got into his chariot and went to Jezreel since Joram was laid up there and King Ahaziah of Judah had gone down to visit Joram. ¹⁷ Now the watchman was standing on the tower in Jezreel. He saw Jehu's mob approaching and shouted, "I see a mob!"

Joram responded, "Choose a rider and send him to meet them and have him ask, 'Do you come in peace?'"

¹⁸ So a horseman went to meet Jehu and said, "This is what the king asks: 'Do you come in peace?'"

Jehu replied, "What do you have to do with peace? Fall in behind me."

The watchman reported, "The messenger reached them but hasn't started back."

¹⁹ So he sent out a second horseman, who went to them and said, "This is what the king asks: 'Do you come in peace?'"

Jehu answered, "What do you have to do with peace? Fall in behind me."

²⁰ Again the watchman reported, "He reached them but hasn't started back. Also, the driving is like that of Jehu son of Nimshi—he drives like a madman."

²¹ "Get the chariot ready!" Joram shouted, and they got it ready. Then King Joram of Israel and King Ahaziah of Judah set out, each in his own chariot, and met Jehu at the plot of

land of Naboth the Jezreelite. ²² When Joram saw Jehu he asked, "Do you come in peace, Jehu?"

He answered, "What peace can there be as long as there is so much prostitution and sorcery from your mother Jezebel?"

²³ Joram turned around and fled, shouting to Ahaziah, "It's treachery, Ahaziah!"

²⁴ Then Jehu drew his bow and shot Joram between the shoulders. The arrow went through his heart, and he slumped down in his chariot. ²⁵ Jehu said to Bidkar his aide, "Pick him up and throw him on the plot of ground belonging to Naboth the Jezreelite. For remember when you and I were riding side by side behind his father Ahab, and the LORD uttered this pronouncement against him: ²⁶ 'As surely as I saw the blood of Naboth and the blood of his sons yesterday'—this is the LORD's declaration—'so will I repay you on this plot of land'—this is the LORD's declaration. So now, according to the word of the LORD, pick him up and throw him on the plot of land."

²⁷ When King Ahaziah of Judah saw what was happening, he fled up the road toward Beth-haggan. Jehu pursued him, shouting, "Shoot him too!" So they shot him in his chariot at Gur Pass near Ibleam, but he fled to Megiddo and died there. ²⁸ Then his servants carried him to Jerusalem in a chariot and buried him in his fathers' tomb in the city of David. ²⁹ It was in the eleventh year of Joram son of Ahab that Ahaziah had become king over Judah.

JEHU KILLS JEZEBEL

³⁰ When Jehu came to Jezreel, Jezebel heard about it, so she painted her eyes, fixed her hair, and looked down from the window. ³¹ As Jehu entered the city gate, she said, "Do you come in peace, Zimri, killer of your master?"

³² He looked up toward the window and said, "Who is on my side? Who?" Two or three eunuchs looked down at him, ³³ and he said, "Throw her down!" So they threw her down, and some of her blood splattered on the wall and on the horses, and Jehu rode over her.

³⁴ Then he went in, ate and drank, and said, "Take care of this cursed woman and bury her, since she's a king's daughter."

³⁵ But when they went out to bury her, they did not find anything but the skull, the feet, and the hands. ³⁶ So they went back and told him, and he said, "This fulfills the LORD's word that he spoke through his servant Elijah the Tishbite: 'In the plot of land at Jezreel, the dogs will eat Jezebel's flesh. ³⁷ Jezebel's corpse will be like manure on the surface of the ground in the plot of land at Jezreel so that no one will be able to say: This is Jezebel.'"

2 Kings 10

JEHU KILLS THE HOUSE OF AHAB

¹ Since Ahab had seventy sons in Samaria, Jehu wrote letters and sent them to Samaria to the rulers of Jezreel, to the elders, and to the guardians of Ahab's sons, saying:

² Your master's sons are with you, and you have chariots, horses, a fortified city, and weaponry, so when this letter arrives ³ select the most qualified of your master's sons, set him on his father's throne, and fight for your master's house.

⁴ However, they were terrified and reasoned, "Look, two kings couldn't stand against him; how can we?"

⁵ So the overseer of the palace, the overseer of the city, the elders, and the guardians sent a message to Jehu: "We are your servants, and we will do whatever you tell us. We will not make anyone king. Do whatever you think is right."

⁶ Then Jehu wrote them a second letter, saying:

If you are on my side, and if you will obey me, bring me the heads of your master's sons at this time tomorrow at Jezreel.

All seventy of the king's sons were being cared for by the city's prominent men. ⁷ When the letter came to them, they took the king's sons and slaughtered all seventy, put their heads in baskets, and sent them to Jehu at Jezreel. ⁸ When the messenger came and told him, "They have brought the heads of the king's sons," the king said, "Pile them in two heaps at the entrance of the city gate until morning."

⁹ The next morning when he went out and stood at the gate, he said to all the people, "You are innocent. It was I

who conspired against my master and killed him. But who struck down all these? [10] Know, then, that not a word the LORD spoke against the house of Ahab will fail, for the LORD has done what he promised through his servant Elijah." [11] So Jehu killed all who remained of the house of Ahab in Jezreel—all his great men, close friends, and priests—leaving him no survivors.

[12] Then he set out and went to Samaria. On the way, while he was at Beth-eked of the Shepherds, [13] Jehu met the relatives of King Ahaziah of Judah and asked, "Who are you?"

They answered, "We're Ahaziah's relatives. We've come down to greet the king's sons and the queen mother's sons."

[14] Then Jehu ordered, "Take them alive." So they took them alive and then slaughtered them at the pit of Beth-eked—forty-two men. He didn't spare any of them.

[15] When he left there, he found Jehonadab son of Rechab coming to meet him. He greeted him and then asked, "Is your heart one with mine?"

"It is," Jehonadab replied.

Jehu said, "If it is, give me your hand."

So he gave him his hand, and Jehu pulled him up into the chariot with him. [16] Then he said, "Come with me and see my zeal for the LORD!" So he let him ride with him in his chariot. [17] When Jehu came to Samaria, he struck down all who remained from the house of Ahab in Samaria until he had annihilated his house, according to the word of the LORD spoken to Elijah.

JEHU KILLS THE BAAL WORSHIPERS

[18] Then Jehu brought all the people together and said to them, "Ahab served Baal a little, but Jehu will serve him a lot. [19] Now, therefore, summon to me all the prophets of Baal, all his servants, and all his priests. None must be missing, for I have a great sacrifice for Baal. Whoever is missing will not live." However, Jehu was acting deceptively in order to destroy the servants of Baal. [20] Jehu commanded, "Consecrate a solemn assembly for Baal." So they called one.

[21] Then Jehu sent messengers throughout all Israel, and all the servants of Baal came; no one failed to come. They entered the temple of Baal, and it was filled from one end to the other. [22] Then he said to the custodian of the wardrobe, "Bring out the garments for all the servants of Baal." So he brought out their garments.

[23] Then Jehu and Jehonadab son of Rechab entered the temple of Baal, and Jehu said to the servants of Baal, "Look carefully to see that there are no servants of the LORD here among you—only servants of Baal." [24] Then they went in to offer sacrifices and burnt offerings.

Now Jehu had stationed eighty men outside, and he warned them, "Whoever allows any of the men I am placing in your hands to escape will forfeit his life for theirs." [25] When he finished offering the burnt offering, Jehu said to the guards and officers, "Go in and kill them. Don't let anyone out." So they struck them down with the sword. Then the guards and officers threw the bodies out and went into the inner room of the temple of Baal. [26] They brought out the pillar of the temple of Baal and burned it, [27] and they tore down the pillar of Baal. Then they tore down the temple of Baal and made it a latrine—which it still is today.

EVALUATION OF JEHU'S REIGN

[28] Jehu eliminated Baal worship from Israel, [29] but he did not turn away from the sins that Jeroboam son of Nebat had caused Israel to commit—worshiping the gold calves that were in Bethel and Dan. [30] Nevertheless, the LORD said to Jehu, "Because you have done well in carrying out what is right in my sight and have done to the house of Ahab all that was in my heart, four generations of your sons will sit on the throne of Israel."

[31] Yet Jehu was not careful to follow the instruction of the LORD God of Israel with all his heart. He did not turn from the sins that Jeroboam had caused Israel to commit.

[32] In those days the LORD began to reduce the size of Israel. Hazael defeated the Israelites throughout their territory [33] from the Jordan eastward: the whole land of Gilead—the Gadites, the Reubenites, and the Manassites—from Aroer which is by the Arnon Valley through Gilead to Bashan.

³⁴ The rest of the events of Jehu's reign, along with all his accomplishments and all his might, are written in the Historical Record of Israel's Kings. ³⁵ Jehu rested with his fathers and was buried in Samaria. His son Jehoahaz became king in his place. ³⁶ The length of Jehu's reign over Israel in Samaria was twenty-eight years.

Psalm 72

A PRAYER FOR THE KING

Of Solomon.

¹ God, give your justice to the king
and your righteousness to the king's son.
² He will judge your people with righteousness
and your afflicted ones with justice.
³ May the mountains bring well-being to the people
and the hills, righteousness.
⁴ May he vindicate the afflicted among the people,
help the poor,
and crush the oppressor.

⁵ May they fear you while the sun endures
and as long as the moon, throughout all generations.
⁶ May the king be like rain that falls on the cut grass,
like spring showers that water the earth.

⁷ May the righteous flourish
in his days
and well-being abound
until the moon is no more.

⁸ May he rule from sea to sea
and from the Euphrates
to the ends of the earth.
⁹ May desert tribes kneel before him
and his enemies lick the dust.
¹⁰ May the kings of Tarshish
and the coasts and islands bring tribute,
the kings of Sheba and Seba offer gifts.
¹¹ Let all kings bow in homage to him,
all nations serve him.

¹² For he will rescue the poor who cry out
and the afflicted who have no helper.
¹³ He will have pity on the poor and helpless
and save the lives of the poor.
¹⁴ He will redeem them from oppression and violence,
for their lives are precious in his sight.

¹⁵ May he live long!
May gold from Sheba be given to him.
May prayer be offered for him continually,
and may he be blessed all day long.
¹⁶ May there be plenty of grain in the land;
may it wave on the tops of the mountains.
May its crops be like Lebanon.
May people flourish in the cities
like the grass of the field.
¹⁷ May his name endure forever;
as long as the sun shines,
may his fame increase.
May all nations be blessed by him
and call him blessed.

¹⁸ Blessed be the LORD God, the God of Israel,
who alone does wonders.
¹⁹ Blessed be his glorious name forever;
the whole earth is filled with his glory.
Amen and amen.
²⁰ The prayers of David son of Jesse are concluded.

NOTES

Come with me and see my zeal for the Lord!

2 KINGS 10:16

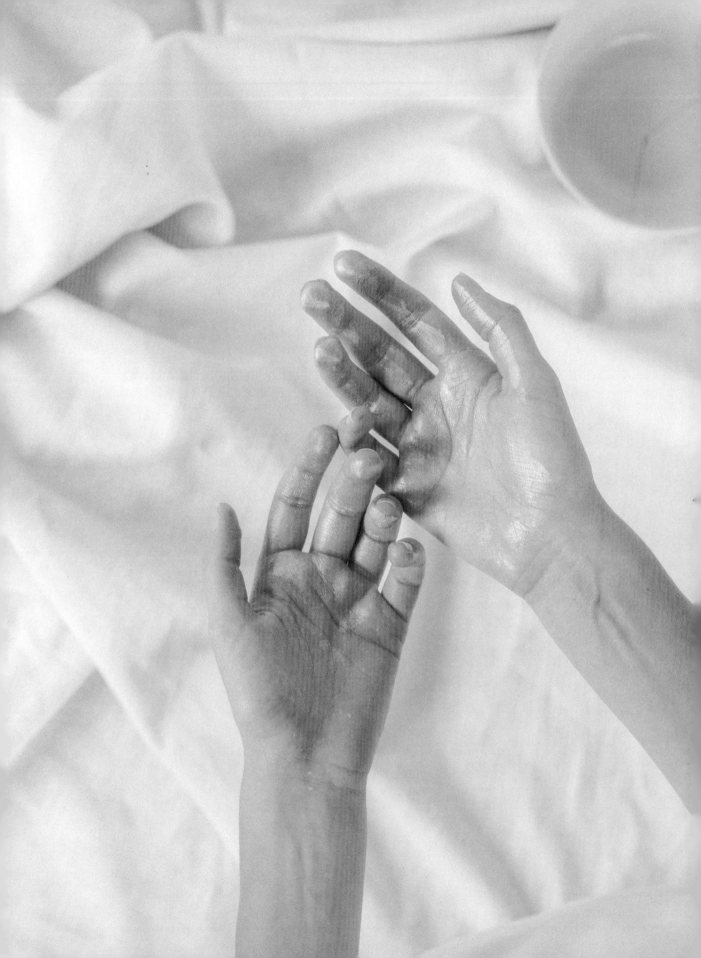

Further Attempts at Reform

2 Kings 11

ATHALIAH USURPS THE THRONE

¹ When Athaliah, Ahaziah's mother, saw that her son was dead, she proceeded to annihilate all the royal heirs. ² Jehosheba, who was King Jehoram's daughter and Ahaziah's sister, secretly rescued Joash son of Ahaziah from among the king's sons who were being killed and put him and the one who nursed him in a bedroom. So he was hidden from Athaliah and was not killed. ³ Joash was in hiding with her in the Lord's temple six years while Athaliah reigned over the land.

ATHALIAH OVERTHROWN

⁴ In the seventh year, Jehoiada sent for the commanders of hundreds, the Carites, and the guards. He had them come to him in the Lord's temple, where he made a covenant with them and put them under oath. He showed them the king's son ⁵ and commanded them, "This is what you are to do: A third of you who come on duty on the Sabbath are to provide protection for the king's palace. ⁶ A third are to be at the Foundation Gate and a third at the gate behind the guards. You are to take turns providing protection for the palace.

⁷ "Your two divisions that go off duty on the Sabbath are to provide the king protection at the Lord's temple. ⁸ Completely surround the king with weapons in hand. Anyone who approaches the ranks is to be put to death. Be with the king in all his daily tasks."

⁹ So the commanders of hundreds did everything the priest Jehoiada commanded. They each brought their men—those coming on duty on the Sabbath and those going off duty—and came to the priest Jehoiada. ¹⁰ The priest gave to the commanders of hundreds King David's spears and shields that were in the Lord's temple. ¹¹ Then the guards stood with their weapons in hand surrounding the king—from the right side of the temple to the left side, by the altar and by the temple.

¹² Jehoiada brought out the king's son, put the crown on him, gave him the testimony, and made him king. They anointed him and clapped their hands and cried, "Long live the king!"

¹³ When Athaliah heard the noise from the guard and the crowd, she went out to the people at the Lord's temple. ¹⁴ She looked, and there was the king standing by the pillar according to the custom. The commanders and the trumpeters were by the king, and all the people of the land were rejoicing and blowing trumpets. Athaliah tore her clothes and screamed "Treason! Treason!"

> Then Jehoiada made a covenant between the LORD, the king, and the people that they would be the LORD's people . . .

[15] Then the priest Jehoiada ordered the commanders of hundreds in charge of the army, "Take her out between the ranks, and put to death by the sword anyone who follows her," for the priest had said, "She is not to be put to death in the LORD's temple." [16] So they arrested her, and she went through the horse entrance to the king's palace, where she was put to death.

JEHOIADA'S REFORMS

[17] Then Jehoiada made a covenant between the LORD, the king, and the people that they would be the LORD's people and another covenant between the king and the people. [18] So all the people of the land went to the temple of Baal and tore it down. They smashed its altars and images to pieces, and they killed Mattan, the priest of Baal, at the altars.

Then Jehoiada the priest appointed guards for the LORD's temple. [19] He took the commanders of hundreds, the Carites, the guards, and all the people of the land, and they brought the king from the LORD's temple. They entered the king's palace by way of the guards' gate. Then Joash sat on the throne of the kings. [20] All the people of the land rejoiced, and the city was quiet, for they had put Athaliah to death by the sword in the king's palace.

JUDAH'S KING JOASH

[21] Joash was seven years old when he became king.

2 Kings 12

[1] In the seventh year of Jehu, Joash became king, and he reigned forty years in Jerusalem. His mother's name was Zibiah; she was from Beer-sheba. [2] Throughout the time the priest Jehoiada instructed him, Joash did what was right in the LORD's sight. [3] Yet the high places were not taken away; the people continued sacrificing and burning incense on the high places.

REPAIRING THE TEMPLE

[4] Then Joash said to the priests, "All the dedicated silver brought to the LORD's temple, census silver, silver from vows, and all silver voluntarily given for the LORD's temple— [5] each priest is to take it from his assessor and repair whatever damage is found in the temple."

[6] But by the twenty-third year of the reign of King Joash, the priests had not repaired the damage to the temple. [7] So King Joash called the priest Jehoiada and the other priests and asked, "Why haven't you repaired the temple's damage? Since you haven't, don't take any silver from your assessors; instead, hand it over for the repair of the temple." [8] So the priests agreed that they would receive no silver from the people and would not be the ones to repair the temple's damage.

⁹ Then the priest Jehoiada took a chest, bored a hole in its lid, and set it beside the altar on the right side as one enters the Lord's temple; the priests who guarded the threshold put into the chest all the silver that was brought to the Lord's temple. ¹⁰ Whenever they saw there was a large amount of silver in the chest, the king's secretary and the high priest would go bag up and tally the silver found in the Lord's temple. ¹¹ Then they would give the weighed silver to those doing the work—those who oversaw the Lord's temple. They in turn would pay it out to those working on the Lord's temple—the carpenters, the builders, ¹² the masons, and the stonecutters—and would use it to buy timber and quarried stone to repair the damage to the Lord's temple and for all expenses for temple repairs.

¹³ However, no silver bowls, wick trimmers, sprinkling basins, trumpets, or any articles of gold or silver were made for the Lord's temple from the contributions brought to the Lord's temple. ¹⁴ Instead, it was given to those doing the work, and they repaired the Lord's temple with it. ¹⁵ No accounting was required from the men who received the silver to pay those doing the work, since they worked with integrity. ¹⁶ The silver from the guilt offering and the sin offering was not brought to the Lord's temple since it belonged to the priests.

ARAMEAN INVASION OF JUDAH

¹⁷ At that time King Hazael of Aram marched up and fought against Gath and captured it. Then he planned to attack Jerusalem. ¹⁸ So King Joash of Judah took all the items consecrated by himself and by his ancestors—Judah's kings Jehoshaphat, Jehoram, and Ahaziah—as well as all the gold found in the treasuries of the Lord's temple and in the king's palace, and he sent them to King Hazael of Aram. Then Hazael withdrew from Jerusalem.

JOASH ASSASSINATED

¹⁹ The rest of the events of Joash's reign, along with all his accomplishments, are written in the Historical Record of Judah's Kings. ²⁰ Joash's servants conspired against him and attacked him at Beth-millo on the road that goes down to Silla. ²¹ It was his servants Jozabad son of Shimeath and Jehozabad son of Shomer who attacked him. He died and they buried him with his fathers in the city of David, and his son Amaziah became king in his place.

ISRAEL'S KING JEHOAHAZ

¹ In the twenty-third year of Judah's King Joash son of Ahaziah, Jehoahaz son of Jehu became king over Israel in Samaria, and he reigned seventeen years. ² He did what was evil in the Lord's sight and followed the sins that Jeroboam son of Nebat had caused Israel to commit; he did not turn away from them. ³ So the Lord's anger burned against Israel, and he handed them over to King Hazael of Aram and to his son Ben-hadad during their reigns.

⁴ Then Jehoahaz sought the Lord's favor, and the Lord's heard him, for he saw the oppression the king of Aram inflicted on Israel. ⁵ Therefore, the Lord gave Israel a deliverer, and they escaped from the power of the Arameans. Then the people of Israel returned to their former way of life, ⁶ but they didn't turn away from the sins that the house of Jeroboam had caused Israel to commit. Jehoahaz continued them, and the Asherah pole also remained standing in Samaria. ⁷ Jehoahaz did not have an army left, except for fifty horsemen, ten chariots, and ten thousand foot soldiers, because the king of Aram had destroyed them, making them like dust at threshing.

⁸ The rest of the events of Jehoahaz's reign, along with all his accomplishments and his might, are written in the Historical Record of Israel's Kings. ⁹ Jehoahaz rested with his fathers, and he was buried in Samaria. His son Jehoash became king in his place.

ISRAEL'S KING JEHOASH

¹⁰ In the thirty-seventh year of Judah's King Joash, Jehoash son of Jehoahaz became king over Israel in Samaria, and he reigned sixteen years. ¹¹ He did what was evil in the Lord's sight. He did not turn away from all the sins that Jeroboam son of Nebat had caused Israel to commit, but he continued them.

¹² The rest of the events of Jehoash's reign, along with all his accomplishments and the power he had to wage war against Judah's King Amaziah, are written in the Historical Record of Israel's Kings. ¹³ Jehoash rested with his fathers, and Jeroboam sat on his throne. Jehoash was buried in Samaria with the kings of Israel.

ELISHA'S DEATH

[14] When Elisha became sick with the illness from which he died, King Jehoash of Israel went down and wept over him and said, "My father, my father, the chariots and horsemen of Israel!"

[15] Elisha responded, "Get a bow and arrows." So he got a bow and arrows. [16] Then Elisha said to the king of Israel, "Grasp the bow." So the king grasped it, and Elisha put his hands on the king's hands. [17] Elisha said, "Open the east window." So he opened it. Elisha said, "Shoot!" So he shot. Then Elisha said, "The LORD's arrow of victory, yes, the arrow of victory over Aram. You are to strike down the Arameans in Aphek until you have put an end to them."

[18] Then Elisha said, "Take the arrows!" So he took them. Then Elisha said to the king of Israel, "Strike the ground!" So he struck the ground three times and stopped. [19] The man of God was angry with him and said, "You should have struck the ground five or six times. Then you would have struck down Aram until you had put an end to them, but now you will strike down Aram only three times." [20] Then Elisha died and was buried.

Now Moabite raiders used to come into the land in the spring of the year. [21] Once, as the Israelites were burying a man, suddenly they saw a raiding party, so they threw the man into Elisha's tomb. When he touched Elisha's bones, the man revived and stood up!

GOD'S MERCY ON ISRAEL

[22] King Hazael of Aram oppressed Israel throughout the reign of Jehoahaz, [23] but the LORD was gracious to them, had compassion on them, and turned toward them because of his covenant with Abraham, Isaac, and Jacob. He was not willing to destroy them. Even now he has not banished them from his presence.

[24] King Hazael of Aram died, and his son Ben-hadad became king in his place. [25] Then Jehoash son of Jehoahaz took back from Ben-hadad son of Hazael the cities that Hazael had taken in war from Jehoash's father Jehoahaz. Jehoash defeated Ben-hadad three times and recovered the cities of Israel.

Psalm 125

ISRAEL'S STABILITY

A song of ascents.

[1] Those who trust in the LORD are like Mount Zion.
It cannot be shaken; it remains forever.
[2] The mountains surround Jerusalem
and the LORD surrounds his people,
both now and forever.

[3] The scepter of the wicked will not remain
over the land allotted to the righteous,
so that the righteous will not apply their hands to injustice.
[4] Do what is good, LORD, to the good,
to those whose hearts are upright.
[5] But as for those who turn aside to crooked ways,
the LORD will banish them with the evildoers.
Peace be with Israel.

NOTES

Even now he has not banished them from his presence.

2 KINGS 13:23

Flawed Kings and Kingdoms

Amaziah, Jehoash, Jeroboam II, Azariah,
Zechariah, Shallum, Menahem, Pekahiah,
Pekah, Jotham

Judah, Israel

2 Kings 14

JUDAH'S KING AMAZIAH

¹ In the second year of Israel's King Jehoash son of Jehoahaz, Amaziah son of Joash became king of Judah. ² He was twenty-five years old when he became king, and he reigned twenty-nine years in Jerusalem. His mother's name was Jehoaddan; she was from Jerusalem. ³ He did what was right in the LORD's sight, but not like his ancestor David. He did everything his father Joash had done. ⁴ Yet the high places were not taken away, and the people continued sacrificing and burning incense on the high places.

⁵ As soon as the kingdom was firmly in his grasp, Amaziah killed his servants who had killed his father the king. ⁶ However, he did not put the children of the killers to death, as it is written in the book of the law of Moses where the LORD commanded, "Fathers are not to be put to death because of children, and children are not to be put to death because of fathers; instead, each one will be put to death for his own sin."

⁷ Amaziah killed ten thousand Edomites in Salt Valley. He took Sela in battle and called it Joktheel, which is still its name today. ⁸ Amaziah then sent messengers to Jehoash son of Jehoahaz, son of Jehu, king of Israel, and challenged him: "Come, let's meet face to face."

⁹ King Jehoash of Israel sent word to King Amaziah of Judah, saying, "The thistle in Lebanon once sent a message to the cedar in Lebanon, saying, 'Give your daughter to my son as a wife.' Then a wild animal in Lebanon passed by and trampled the thistle. ¹⁰ You have indeed defeated Edom, and you have become overconfident. Enjoy your glory and stay at home. Why should you stir up such trouble that you fall—you and Judah with you?"

¹¹ But Amaziah would not listen, so King Jehoash of Israel advanced. He and King Amaziah of Judah met face to face at Beth-shemesh that belonged to Judah. ¹² Judah was routed before Israel, and each man fled to his own tent. ¹³ King Jehoash of Israel captured Judah's King Amaziah son of Joash, son of Ahaziah, at Beth-shemesh. Then Jehoash went to Jerusalem and broke down two hundred yards of Jerusalem's wall from the Ephraim Gate to the Corner Gate. ¹⁴ He took all the gold and silver, all the articles found in the LORD's temple and in the treasuries of the king's palace, and some hostages. Then he returned to Samaria.

JEHOASH'S DEATH

¹⁵ The rest of the events of Jehoash's reign, along with his accomplishments, his might, and how he waged war against King Amaziah of Judah, are

written in the Historical Record of Israel's Kings. ¹⁶ Jehoash rested with his fathers, and he was buried in Samaria with the kings of Israel. His son Jeroboam became king in his place.

AMAZIAH'S DEATH

¹⁷ Judah's King Amaziah son of Joash lived fifteen years after the death of Israel's King Jehoash son of Jehoahaz. ¹⁸ The rest of the events of Amaziah's reign are written in the Historical Record of Judah's Kings. ¹⁹ A conspiracy was formed against him in Jerusalem, and he fled to Lachish. However, men were sent after him to Lachish, and they put him to death there. ²⁰ They carried him back on horses, and he was buried in Jerusalem with his fathers in the city of David.

²¹ Then all the people of Judah took Azariah, who was sixteen years old, and made him king in place of his father Amaziah. ²² After Amaziah the king rested with his fathers, Azariah rebuilt Elath and restored it to Judah.

ISRAEL'S KING JEROBOAM

²³ In the fifteenth year of Judah's King Amaziah son of Joash, Jeroboam son of Jehoash became king of Israel in Samaria, and he reigned forty-one years. ²⁴ He did what was evil in the LORD's sight. He did not turn away from all the sins Jeroboam son of Nebat had caused Israel to commit.

²⁵ He restored Israel's border from Lebo-hamath as far as the Sea of the Arabah, according to the word the LORD, the God of Israel, had spoken through his servant, the prophet Jonah son of Amittai from Gath-hepher. ²⁶ For the LORD saw that the affliction of Israel was very bitter for both slaves and free people. There was no one to help Israel. ²⁷ The LORD had not said he would blot out the name of Israel under heaven, so he delivered them by the hand of Jeroboam son of Jehoash.

²⁸ The rest of the events of Jeroboam's reign—along with all his accomplishments, the power he had to wage war, and how he recovered for Israel Damascus and Hamath, which had belonged to Judah —are written in the Historical Record of Israel's Kings. ²⁹ Jeroboam rested with his fathers, the kings of Israel. His son Zechariah became king in his place.

2 Kings 15

JUDAH'S KING AZARIAH

¹ In the twenty-seventh year of Israel's King Jeroboam, Azariah son of Amaziah became king of Judah. ² He was sixteen years old when he became king, and he reigned fifty-two years in Jerusalem. His mother's name was Jecoliah; she was from Jerusalem. ³ Azariah did what was right in the LORD's sight just as his father Amaziah had done. ⁴ Yet the high places were not taken away; the people continued sacrificing and burning incense on the high places.

⁵ The LORD afflicted the king, and he had a serious skin disease until the day of his death. He lived in quarantine, while Jotham, the king's son, was over the household governing the people of the land.

⁶ The rest of the events of Azariah's reign, along with all his accomplishments, are written in the Historical Record of Judah's Kings. ⁷ Azariah rested with his fathers and was buried with his fathers in the city of David. His son Jotham became king in his place.

ISRAEL'S KING ZECHARIAH

⁸ In the thirty-eighth year of Judah's King Azariah, Zechariah son of Jeroboam reigned over Israel in Samaria for six months. ⁹ He did what was evil in the LORD's sight as his fathers had done. He did not turn away from the sins Jeroboam son of Nebat had caused Israel to commit.

¹⁰ Shallum son of Jabesh conspired against Zechariah. He struck him down publicly, killed him, and became king in his place. ¹¹ As for the rest of the events of Zechariah's reign, they are written in the Historical Record of Israel's Kings. ¹² The word of the LORD that he spoke to Jehu was, "Four generations of your sons will sit on the throne of Israel," and it was so.

ISRAEL'S KING SHALLUM

¹³ In the thirty-ninth year of Judah's King Uzziah, Shallum son of Jabesh became king; he reigned in Samaria a full month. ¹⁴ Then Menahem son of Gadi came up from Tirzah to Samaria and struck down Shallum son of Jabesh there. He

killed him and became king in his place. ¹⁵ As for the rest of the events of Shallum's reign, along with the conspiracy that he formed, they are written in the Historical Record of Israel's Kings.

ISRAEL'S KING MENAHEM

¹⁶ At that time, starting from Tirzah, Menahem attacked Tiphsah, all who were in it, and its territory because they wouldn't surrender. He ripped open all the pregnant women.

¹⁷ In the thirty-ninth year of Judah's King Azariah, Menahem son of Gadi became king over Israel, and he reigned ten years in Samaria. ¹⁸ He did what was evil in the LORD's sight. Throughout his reign, he did not turn away from the sins Jeroboam son of Nebat had caused Israel to commit.

¹⁹ King Pul of Assyria invaded the land, so Menahem gave Pul seventy-five thousand pounds of silver so that Pul would support him to strengthen his grasp on the kingdom. ²⁰ Then Menahem exacted twenty ounces of silver from each of the prominent men of Israel to give to the king of Assyria. So the king of Assyria withdrew and did not stay there in the land.

²¹ The rest of the events of Menahem's reign, along with all his accomplishments, are written in the Historical Record of Israel's Kings. ²² Menahem rested with his fathers, and his son Pekahiah became king in his place.

ISRAEL'S KING PEKAHIAH

²³ In the fiftieth year of Judah's King Azariah, Pekahiah son of Menahem became king over Israel in Samaria, and he reigned two years. ²⁴ He did what was evil in the LORD's sight and did not turn away from the sins Jeroboam son of Nebat had caused Israel to commit.

²⁵ Then his officer, Pekah son of Remaliah, conspired against him and struck him down in Samaria at the citadel of the king's palace —with Argob and Arieh. There were fifty Gileadite men with Pekah. He killed Pekahiah and became king in his place.

²⁶ As for the rest of the events of Pekahiah's reign, along with all his accomplishments, they are written in the Historical Record of Israel's Kings.

ISRAEL'S KING PEKAH

²⁷ In the fifty-second year of Judah's King Azariah, Pekah son of Remaliah became king over Israel in Samaria, and he reigned twenty years. ²⁸ He did what was evil in the LORD's sight. He did not turn away from the sins Jeroboam son of Nebat had caused Israel to commit.

²⁹ In the days of King Pekah of Israel, **King Tiglath-pileser** of Assyria came and captured Ijon, Abel-beth-maacah, Janoah, Kedesh, Hazor, Gilead, and Galilee—all the land of Naphtali—and deported the people to Assyria.

³⁰ Then Hoshea son of Elah organized a conspiracy against Pekah son of Remaliah. He attacked him, killed him, and became king in his place in the twentieth year of Jotham son of Uzziah.

³¹ As for the rest of the events of Pekah's reign, along with all his accomplishments, they are written in the Historical Record of Israel's Kings.

JUDAH'S KING JOTHAM

³² In the second year of Israel's King Pekah son of Remaliah, Jotham son of Uzziah became king of Judah. ³³ He was twenty-five years old when he became king, and he reigned sixteen years in Jerusalem. His mother's name was Jerusha daughter of Zadok. ³⁴ He did what was right in the LORD's sight just as his father Uzziah had done. ³⁵ Yet the high places were not taken away; the people continued sacrificing and burning incense on the high places.

Jotham built the Upper Gate of the LORD's temple. ³⁶ The rest of the events of Jotham's reign, along with all his accomplishments, are written in the Historical Record of Judah's Kings. ³⁷ In those days the LORD began sending Aram's **King Rezin** and Pekah son of Remaliah against Judah. ³⁸ Jotham rested with his fathers and was buried with his fathers in the city of his ancestor David. His son Ahaz became king in his place.

Ezekiel 37:1-14

THE VALLEY OF DRY BONES

¹ The hand of the LORD was on me, and he brought me out by his Spirit and set me down in the middle of the valley; it was full of bones. ² He led me all around them. There were a great many of them on the surface of the valley, and they were very dry. ³ Then he said to me, "Son of man, can these bones live?"

I replied, "Lord GOD, only you know."

⁴ He said to me, "Prophesy concerning these bones and say to them: Dry bones, hear the word of the LORD! ⁵ This is what the Lord GOD says to these bones: I will cause breath to enter you, and you will live. ⁶ I will put tendons on you, make flesh grow on you, and cover you with skin. I will put breath in you so that you come to life. Then you will know that I am the LORD."

⁷ So I prophesied as I had been commanded. While I was prophesying, there was a noise, a rattling sound, and the bones came together, bone to bone. ⁸ As I looked, tendons appeared on them, flesh grew, and skin covered them, but there was no breath in them. ⁹ He said to me, "Prophesy to the breath, prophesy, son of man. Say to it: This is what the Lord GOD says: Breath, come from the four winds and breathe into these slain so that they may live!" ¹⁰ So I prophesied as he commanded me; the breath entered them, and they came to life and stood on their feet, a vast army.

¹¹ Then he said to me, "Son of man, these bones are the whole house of Israel. Look how they say, 'Our bones are dried up, and our hope has perished; we are cut off.' ¹² Therefore, prophesy and say to them: This is what the Lord GOD says: I am going to open your graves and bring you up from them, my people, and lead you into the land of Israel. ¹³ You will know that I am the LORD, my people, when I open your graves and bring you up from them. ¹⁴ I will put my Spirit in you, and you will live, and I will settle you in your own land. Then you will know that I am the LORD. I have spoken, and I will do it. This is the declaration of the LORD.'"

Luke 5:32

"I have not come to call the righteous, but sinners to repentance."

NOTES

There was no one to help Israel.

2 KINGS 14:26

Grace Day

DAY 20   Use this day to pray, rest, and reflect on this week's
reading, giving thanks for the grace that is ours in Christ.

Blessed be the LORD God, the God
of Israel, who alone does wonders.
Blessed be his glorious name
forever; the whole earth is filled
with his glory. Amen and amen.

PSALM 72:18-19

DATE

WEEKLY

DAY · · · 21

TRUTH

Scripture is God-breathed and true. When we memorize it, we carry the gospel with us wherever we go.

This week we will memorize the key verse for 2 Kings, a reminder of the Lord's faithfulness to His people.

Find the corresponding memory card in the back of this book.

For the sake of his servant David, the LORD was unwilling to destroy Judah...

2 KINGS 8:19a

The Fall of Israel

2 Kings 16

JUDAH'S KING AHAZ

¹ In the seventeenth year of Pekah son of Remaliah, Ahaz son of Jotham became king of Judah. ² Ahaz was twenty years old when he became king, and he reigned sixteen years in Jerusalem. He did not do what was right in the sight of the LORD his God like his ancestor David ³ but walked in the ways of the kings of Israel. He even sacrificed his son in the fire, imitating the detestable practices of the nations the LORD had dispossessed before the Israelites. ⁴ He sacrificed and burned incense on the high places, on the hills, and under every green tree.

⁵ Then Aram's King Rezin and Israel's King Pekah son of Remaliah came to wage war against Jerusalem. They besieged Ahaz but were not able to conquer him. ⁶ At that time Aram's King Rezin recovered Elath for Aram and expelled the Judahites from Elath. Then the Arameans came to Elath, and they still live there today.

⁷ So Ahaz sent messengers to King Tiglath-pileser of Assyria, saying, "I am your servant and your son. March up and save me from the grasp of the king of Aram and of the king of Israel, who are rising up against me." ⁸ Ahaz also took the silver and gold found in the LORD's temple and in the treasuries of the king's palace and sent them to the king of Assyria as a bribe. ⁹ So the king of Assyria listened to him and marched up to Damascus and captured it. He deported its people to Kir but put Rezin to death.

AHAZ'S IDOLATRY

¹⁰ King Ahaz went to Damascus to meet King Tiglath-pileser of Assyria. When he saw the altar that was in Damascus, King Ahaz sent a model of the altar and complete plans for its construction to the priest Uriah. ¹¹ Uriah built the altar according to all the instructions King Ahaz sent from Damascus. Therefore, by the time King Ahaz came back from Damascus, the priest Uriah had completed it. ¹² When the king came back from Damascus, he saw the altar. Then he approached the altar and ascended it. ¹³ He offered his burnt offering and his grain offering, poured out his drink offering, and splattered the blood of his fellowship offerings on the altar. ¹⁴ He took the bronze altar that was before the LORD in front of the temple between his altar and the LORD's temple, and put it on the north side of his altar.

¹⁵ Then King Ahaz commanded the priest Uriah, "Offer on the great altar the morning burnt offering, the evening grain

offering, and the king's burnt offering and his grain offering. Also offer the burnt offering of all the people of the land, their grain offering, and their drink offerings. Splatter on the altar all the blood of the burnt offering and all the blood of sacrifice. The bronze altar will be for me to seek guidance." ¹⁶ The priest Uriah did everything King Ahaz commanded.

¹⁷ Then King Ahaz cut off the frames of the water carts and removed the bronze basin from each of them. He took the basin from the bronze oxen that were under it and put it on a stone pavement. ¹⁸ To satisfy the king of Assyria, he removed from the LORD's temple the Sabbath canopy they had built in the palace, and he closed the outer entrance for the king.

AHAZ'S DEATH

¹⁹ The rest of the events of Ahaz's reign, along with his accomplishments, are written in the Historical Record of Judah's Kings. ²⁰ Ahaz rested with his fathers and was buried with his fathers in the city of David, and his son Hezekiah became king in his place.

2 Kings 17

ISRAEL'S KING HOSHEA

¹ In the twelfth year of Judah's King Ahaz, Hoshea son of Elah became king over Israel in Samaria, and he reigned nine years. ² He did what was evil in the LORD's sight, but not like the kings of Israel who preceded him.

³ **King Shalmaneser** of Assyria attacked him, and Hoshea became his vassal and paid him tribute. ⁴ But the king of Assyria caught Hoshea in a conspiracy: He had sent envoys to So king of Egypt and had not paid tribute to the king of Assyria as in previous years. Therefore the king of Assyria arrested him and put him in prison. ⁵ The king of Assyria invaded the whole land, marched up to Samaria, and besieged it for three years.

THE FALL OF SAMARIA

⁶ In the ninth year of Hoshea, the king of Assyria captured Samaria. He deported the Israelites to Assyria and settled them in Halah, along the Habor (Gozan's river), and in the cities of the Medes.

WHY ISRAEL FELL

⁷ This disaster happened because the people of Israel sinned against the LORD their God who had brought them out of the land of Egypt from the power of Pharaoh king of Egypt and because they worshiped other gods. ⁸ They lived according to the customs of the nations that the LORD had dispossessed before the Israelites and according to what the kings of Israel did. ⁹ The Israelites secretly did things against the LORD their God that were not right. They built high places in all their towns from watchtower to fortified city. ¹⁰ They set up for themselves sacred pillars and Asherah poles on every high hill and under every green tree. ¹¹ They burned incense there on all the high places just like the nations that the LORD had driven out before them had done. They did evil things, angering the LORD. ¹² They served idols, although the LORD had told them, "You must not do this." ¹³ Still, the LORD warned Israel and Judah through every prophet and every seer, saying, "Turn from your evil ways and keep my commands and statutes according to the whole law I commanded your ancestors and sent to you through my servants the prophets."

¹⁴ But they would not listen. Instead they became obstinate like their ancestors who did not believe the LORD their God. ¹⁵ They rejected his statutes and his covenant he had made with their ancestors and the warnings he had given them. They followed worthless idols and became worthless themselves, following the surrounding nations the LORD had commanded them not to imitate.

¹⁶ They abandoned all the commands of the LORD their God. They made cast images for themselves, two calves, and an Asherah pole. They bowed in worship to all the stars in the sky and served Baal. ¹⁷ They sacrificed their sons and daughters in the fire and practiced divination and interpreted omens. They devoted themselves to do what was evil in the LORD's sight and angered him.

¹⁸ Therefore, the LORD was very angry with Israel, and he removed them from his presence. Only the tribe of Judah remained. ¹⁹ Even Judah did not keep the commands of the LORD their God but lived according to the customs Israel had practiced. ²⁰ So the LORD rejected all the descendants of

Israel, punished them, and handed them over to plunderers until he had banished them from his presence.

SUMMARY OF ISRAEL'S HISTORY

²¹ When the LORD tore Israel from the house of David, Israel made Jeroboam son of Nebat king. Then Jeroboam led Israel away from following the LORD and caused them to commit immense sin. ²² The Israelites persisted in all the sins that Jeroboam committed and did not turn away from them. ²³ Finally, the LORD removed Israel from his presence just as he had declared through all his servants the prophets. So Israel has been exiled to Assyria from their homeland to this very day.

FOREIGN REFUGEES IN ISRAEL

²⁴ Then the king of Assyria brought people from Babylon, Cuthah, Avva, Hamath, and Sepharvaim and settled them in place of the Israelites in the cities of Samaria. The settlers took possession of Samaria and lived in its cities. ²⁵ When they first lived there, they did not fear the LORD. So the LORD sent lions among them, which killed some of them. ²⁶ The settlers said to the king of Assyria, "The nations that you have deported and placed in the cities of Samaria do not know the requirements of the god of the land. Therefore he has sent lions among them that are killing them because the people don't know the requirements of the god of the land."

²⁷ Then the king of Assyria issued a command: "Send back one of the priests you deported. Have him go and live there so he can teach them the requirements of the god of the land." ²⁸ So one of the priests they had deported came and lived in Bethel, and he began to teach them how they should fear the LORD.

²⁹ But the people of each nation were still making their own gods in the cities where they lived and putting them in the shrines of the high places that the people of Samaria had made. ³⁰ The men of Babylon made **Succoth-benoth**, the men of Cuth made **Nergal**, the men of Hamath made **Ashima**, ³¹ the Avvites made **Nibhaz** and **Tartak**, and the Sepharvites burned their children in the fire to **Adrammelech** and **Anammelech**, the gods of Sepharvaim. ³² They feared the LORD, but they also made from their ranks priests for the high places, who were working for them at the shrines of the high places. ³³ They feared the LORD, but they also worshiped their own gods according to the practice of the nations from which they had been deported.

³⁴ They are still observing the former practices to this day. None of them fear the LORD or observe the statutes and ordinances, the law and commandments that the LORD had commanded the descendants of Jacob, whom he had given the name Israel. ³⁵ The LORD made a covenant with Jacob's descendants and commanded them, "Do not fear other gods; do not bow in worship to them; do not serve them; do not sacrifice to them. ³⁶ Instead fear the LORD, who brought you up from the land of Egypt with great power and an outstretched arm. You are to bow down to him, and you are to sacrifice to him. ³⁷ You are to be careful always to observe the statutes, the ordinances, the law, and the commandments he wrote for you; do not fear other gods. ³⁸ Do not forget the covenant that I have made with you. Do not fear other gods, ³⁹ but fear the LORD your God, and he will rescue you from all your enemies."

⁴⁰ However, these nations would not listen but continued observing their former practices. ⁴¹ They feared the LORD but also served their idols. Still today, their children and grandchildren continue doing as their fathers did.

Proverbs 29:2

When the righteous flourish, the people rejoice,
but when the wicked rule, people groan.

1 Peter 2:21–25

²¹ For you were called to this, because Christ also suffered for you, leaving you an example, that you should follow in his steps. ²² He did not commit sin, and no deceit was found in his mouth; ²³ when he was insulted, he did not insult in return; when he suffered, he did not threaten but entrusted himself to the one who judges justly. ²⁴ He himself bore our sins in his body on the tree; so that, having died to sins, we might live for righteousness. By his wounds you have been healed. ²⁵ For you were like sheep going astray, but you have now returned to the Shepherd and Overseer of your souls.

NOTES

But they would not listen. Instead they became obstinate like their ancestors who did not believe the Lord their God.

2 KINGS 17:14

Prophets and Kings of Israel and Judah

The books of 1 and 2 Kings tell the story of God's people from the end of the united kingdom of Israel through the divided kingdoms and eventual exiles. Though many kings reigned during this time, God and His covenant were Israel's ultimate authority. Prophets served as an important foil to the often evil kings of Israel and Judah by holding them accountable to God's Word. They were emissaries from the true King's royal court who spoke on His behalf.

On this timeline of the kings of Israel and Judah, the prophets mentioned in 1 and 2 Kings are included in gold above or below the king or kings they confronted.

KINGS OF THE UNITED KINGDOM OF ISRAEL

ca 1051–1010	ca 1010–970*	ca 971–931
SAUL	DAVID	SOLOMON
	Nathan	Nathan

*David became king of Judah in 1010 BC and over all of Israel in 1003 BC.
**Dates overlap with previous ruler, indicating co-regency.

1000 BC

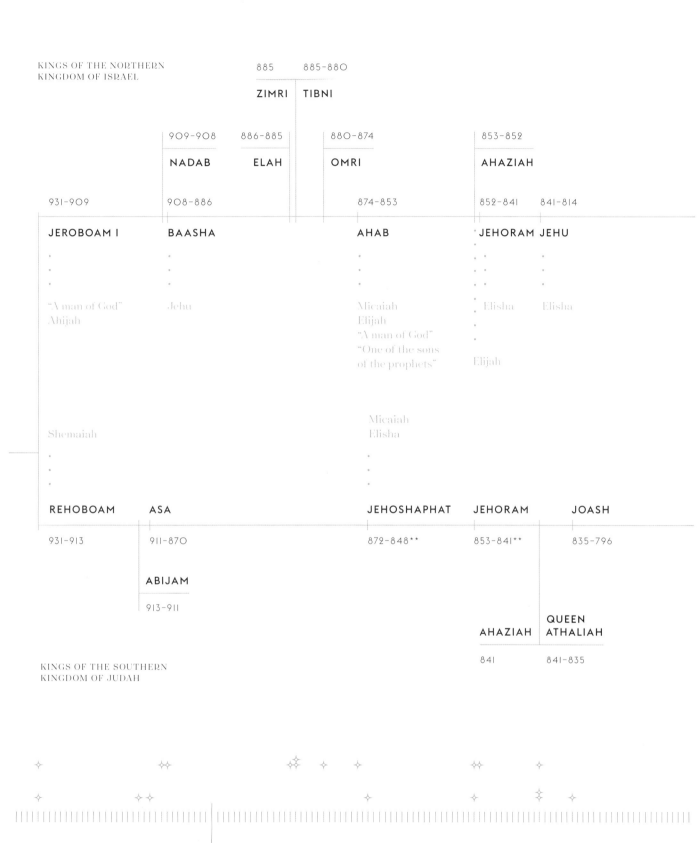

					885	885-880					
					ZIMRI	**TIBNI**					

909-908	886-885		880-874		853-852
NADAB	**ELAH**		**OMRI**		**AHAZIAH**

931-909   908-886   874-853   852-841   841-814

JEROBOAM I   **BAASHA**   **AHAB**   **JEHORAM JEHU**

"A man of God"   Jehu   Micaiah   Elisha   Elisha
Ahijah   Elijah
                                          "A man of God"
                                          "One of the sons
                                          of the prophets"   Elijah

                                          Micaiah
Shemaiah   Elisha

REHOBOAM   **ASA**   **JEHOSHAPHAT**   **JEHORAM**   **JOASH**

931-913   911-870   872-848**   853-841**   835-796

                ABIJAM

                913-911

                                                        AHAZIAH   QUEEN
                                                                       ATHALIAH

                                                        841   841-835

900 BC

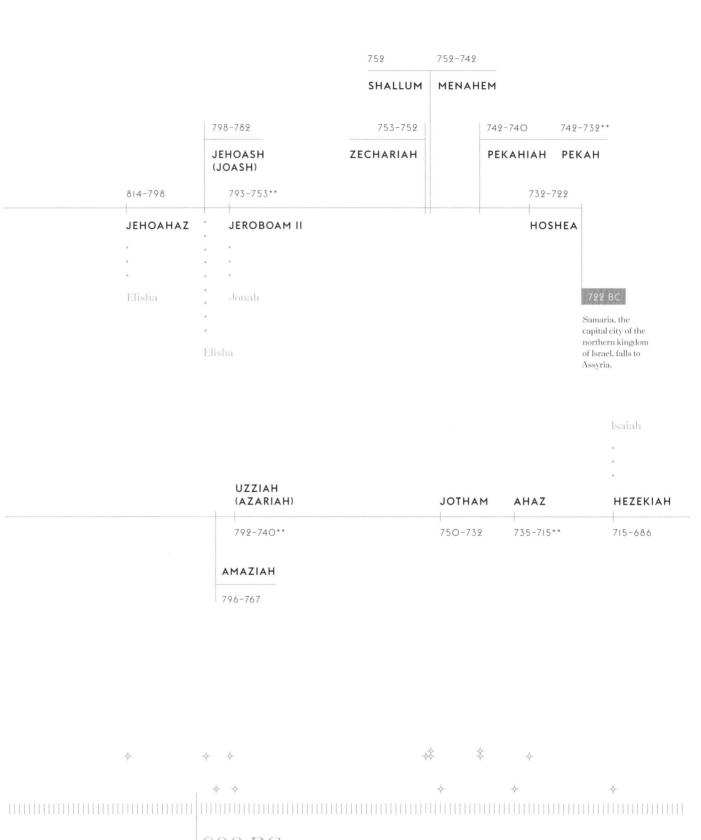

752
SHALLUM

752–742
MENAHEM

798–782
JEHOASH
(JOASH)

753–752
ZECHARIAH

742–740
PEKAHIAH

742–732**
PEKAH

814–798
JEHOAHAZ

793–753**
JEROBOAM II

732–722
HOSHEA

Elisha

Jonah

Elisha

722 BC

Samaria, the
capital city of the
northern kingdom
of Israel, falls to
Assyria.

Isaiah

UZZIAH
(AZARIAH)

JOTHAM

AHAZ

HEZEKIAH

792–740**

750–732

735–715**

715–686

AMAZIAH

796–767

800 BC

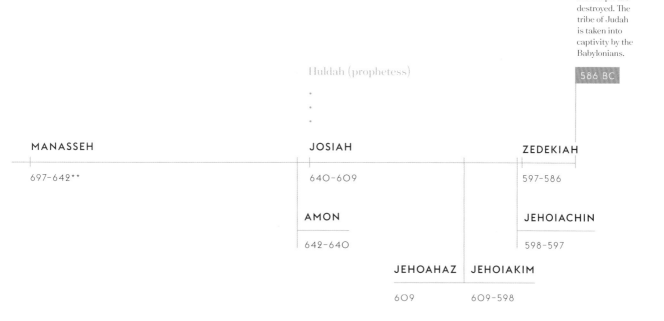

Jerusalem and
the temple are
destroyed. The
tribe of Judah
is taken into
captivity by the
Babylonians.

Huldah (prophetess)

586 BC

MANASSEH

697-642**

JOSIAH

640-609

ZEDEKIAH

597-586

AMON

642-640

JEHOIACHIN

598-597

JEHOAHAZ   JEHOIAKIM

609   609-598

700 BC

600 BC

Hezekiah's Prayer

2 Kings 18

JUDAH'S KING HEZEKIAH

¹ In the third year of Israel's King Hoshea son of Elah, Hezekiah son of Ahaz became king of Judah. ² He was twenty-five years old when he became king, and he reigned twenty-nine years in Jerusalem. His mother's name was Abi daughter of Zechariah. ³ He did what was right in the LORD's sight just as his ancestor David had done. ⁴ He removed the high places, shattered the sacred pillars, and cut down the Asherah poles. He broke into pieces the bronze snake that Moses made, for until then the Israelites were burning incense to it. It was called Nehushtan.

⁵ Hezekiah relied on the LORD God of Israel; not one of the kings of Judah was like him, either before him or after him. ⁶ He remained faithful to the LORD and did not turn from following him but kept the commands the LORD had commanded Moses.

⁷ The LORD was with him, and wherever he went he prospered. He rebelled against the king of Assyria and did not serve him. ⁸ He defeated the Philistines as far as Gaza and its borders, from watchtower to fortified city.

REVIEW OF ISRAEL'S FALL

⁹ In the fourth year of King Hezekiah, which was the seventh year of Israel's King Hoshea son of Elah, Assyria's King Shalmaneser marched against Samaria and besieged it. ¹⁰ The Assyrians captured it at the end of three years. In the sixth year of Hezekiah, which was the ninth year of Israel's King Hoshea, Samaria was captured. ¹¹ The king of Assyria deported the Israelites to Assyria and put them in Halah, along the Habor (Gozan's river), and in the cities of the Medes, ¹² because they did not listen to the LORD their God but violated his covenant—all he had commanded Moses the servant of the LORD. They did not listen, and they did not obey.

SENNACHERIB'S INVASION

¹³ In the fourteenth year of King Hezekiah, Assyria's **King Sennacherib** attacked all the fortified cities of Judah and captured them. ¹⁴ So King Hezekiah of Judah sent word to the king of Assyria at Lachish: "I have done wrong; withdraw from me. Whatever you demand from me, I will pay." The king of Assyria demanded eleven tons of silver and one ton of gold from King Hezekiah of Judah. ¹⁵ So Hezekiah gave him all the silver found in the LORD's temple and in the treasuries of the king's palace.

¹⁶ At that time Hezekiah stripped the gold from the doors of the LORD's sanctuary and from the doorposts he had overlaid and gave it to the king of Assyria.

[17] Then the king of Assyria sent the field marshal, the chief of staff, and his royal spokesman, along with a massive army, from Lachish to King Hezekiah at Jerusalem. They advanced and came to Jerusalem, and they took their position by the aqueduct of the upper pool, by the road to the Launderer's Field. [18] They called for the king, but Eliakim son of Hilkiah, who was in charge of the palace, Shebnah the court secretary, and Joah son of Asaph, the court historian, came out to them.

THE ROYAL SPOKESMAN'S SPEECH

[19] Then the royal spokesman said to them, "Tell Hezekiah this is what the great king, the king of Assyria, says: 'What are you relying on? [20] You think mere words are strategy and strength for war. Who are you now relying on so that you have rebelled against me? [21] Now look, you are relying on Egypt, that splintered reed of a staff that will pierce the hand of anyone who grabs it and leans on it. This is what Pharaoh king of Egypt is to all who rely on him. [22] Suppose you say to me, "We rely on the LORD our God." Isn't he the one whose high places and altars Hezekiah has removed, saying to Judah and to Jerusalem, "You must worship at this altar in Jerusalem"?'

[23] "So now, make a bargain with my master the king of Assyria. I'll give you two thousand horses if you're able to supply riders for them! [24] How then can you drive back a single officer among the least of my master's servants? How can you rely on Egypt for chariots and for horsemen? [25] Now, have I attacked this place to destroy it without the LORD's approval? The LORD said to me, 'Attack this land and destroy it.'"

[26] Then Eliakim son of Hilkiah, Shebnah, and Joah said to the royal spokesman, "Please speak to your servants in Aramaic, since we understand it. Don't speak with us in Hebrew within earshot of the people on the wall."

[27] But the royal spokesman said to them, "Has my master sent me to speak these words only to your master and to you? Hasn't he also sent me to the men who sit on the wall, destined with you to eat their own excrement and drink their own urine?"

[28] The royal spokesman stood and called out loudly in Hebrew: "Hear the word of the great king, the king of Assyria. [29] This is what the king says: 'Don't let Hezekiah deceive you; he can't rescue you from my power. [30] Don't let Hezekiah persuade you to rely on the LORD by saying, "Certainly the LORD will rescue us! This city will not be handed over to the king of Assyria."'

[31] "Don't listen to Hezekiah, for this is what the king of Assyria says: 'Make peace with me and surrender to me. Then each of you may eat from his own vine and his own fig tree, and each may drink water from his own cistern [32] until I come and take you away to a land like your own land— a land of grain and new wine, a land of bread and vineyards, a land of olive trees and honey—so that you may live and not die. But don't listen to Hezekiah when he misleads you, saying, "The LORD will rescue us." [33] Has any of the gods of the nations ever rescued his land from the power of the king of Assyria? [34] Where are the gods of Hamath and Arpad? Where are the gods of Sepharvaim, Hena, and Ivvah? Have they rescued Samaria from my power? [35] Who among all the gods of the lands has rescued his land from my power? So will the LORD rescue Jerusalem from my power?'"

[36] But the people kept silent; they did not answer him at all, for the king's command was, "Don't answer him." [37] Then Eliakim son of Hilkiah, who was in charge of the palace, Shebna the court secretary, and Joah son of Asaph, the court historian, came to Hezekiah with their clothes torn and reported to him the words of the royal spokesman.

2 Kings 19

HEZEKIAH SEEKS ISAIAH'S COUNSEL

[1] When King Hezekiah heard their report, he tore his clothes, covered himself with sackcloth, and went into the LORD's temple. [2] He sent Eliakim, who was in charge of the palace, Shebna the court secretary, and the leading priests, who were wearing sackcloth, to the prophet Isaiah son of Amoz. [3] They said to him, "This is what Hezekiah says: 'Today is a day of distress, rebuke, and disgrace, for children have come to the point of birth, but there is no strength to deliver them. [4] Perhaps the LORD your God will hear all the words of the royal spokesman, whom his master the king of Assyria sent to mock the living God, and will rebuke him for the words that the LORD your God has heard. Therefore, offer a prayer for the surviving remnant.'"

Now, LORD our God, please save us from his power so that all the kingdoms of the earth may know that you, LORD, are God—you alone.

⁵ So the servants of King Hezekiah went to Isaiah, ⁶ who said to them, "Tell your master, 'The LORD says this: Don't be afraid because of the words you have heard, with which the king of Assyria's attendants have blasphemed me. ⁷ I am about to put a spirit in him, and he will hear a rumor and return to his own land, where I will cause him to fall by the sword.'"

SENNACHERIB'S DEPARTING THREAT

⁸ When the royal spokesman heard that the king of Assyria had pulled out of Lachish, he left and found him fighting against Libnah. ⁹ The king had heard concerning King Tirhakah of Cush, "Look, he has set out to fight against you." So he again sent messengers to Hezekiah, saying, ¹⁰ "Say this to King Hezekiah of Judah: 'Don't let your God, on whom you rely, deceive you by promising that Jerusalem will not be handed over to the king of Assyria. ¹¹ Look, you have heard what the kings of Assyria have done to all the countries: They completely destroyed them. Will you be rescued? ¹² Did the gods of the nations that my predecessors destroyed rescue them—nations such as Gozan, Haran, Rezeph, and the Edenites in Telassar? ¹³ Where is the king of Hamath, the king of Arpad, the king of the city of Sepharvaim, Hena, or Ivvah?'"

HEZEKIAH'S PRAYER

¹⁴ Hezekiah took the letter from the messengers' hands, read it, then went up to the LORD's temple, and spread it out before the LORD. ¹⁵ Then Hezekiah prayed before the LORD:

LORD God of Israel, enthroned between the cherubim, you are God—you alone—of all the kingdoms of the earth. You made the heavens and the earth. ¹⁶ Listen closely, LORD, and hear; open your eyes, LORD, and see. Hear the words that Sennacherib has sent to mock the living God. ¹⁷ LORD, it is true that the kings of Assyria have devastated the nations and their lands. ¹⁸ They have thrown their gods into the fire, for they were not gods but made by human hands—wood and stone. So they have destroyed them. ¹⁹ Now, LORD our God, please save us from his power so that all the kingdoms of the earth may know that you, LORD, are God—you alone.

GOD'S ANSWER THROUGH ISAIAH

²⁰ Then Isaiah son of Amoz sent a message to Hezekiah: "The LORD, the God of Israel says, 'I have heard your prayer to me about King Sennacherib of Assyria.' ²¹ This is the word the LORD has spoken against him:

Virgin Daughter Zion
despises you and scorns you;
Daughter Jerusalem
shakes her head behind your back.

²² Who is it you mocked and blasphemed?
Against whom have you raised your voice
and lifted your eyes in pride?
Against the Holy One of Israel!
²³ You have mocked the LORD through your messengers.
You have said, 'With my many chariots
I have gone up to the heights of the mountains,
to the far recesses of Lebanon.
I cut down its tallest cedars,
its choice cypress trees.
I came to its farthest outpost,
its densest forest.
²⁴ I dug wells
and drank water in foreign lands.
I dried up all the streams of Egypt
with the soles of my feet.'

²⁵ Have you not heard?
I designed it long ago;
I planned it in days gone by.
I have now brought it to pass,
and you have crushed fortified cities
into piles of rubble.
²⁶ Their inhabitants have become powerless,
dismayed, and ashamed.
They are plants of the field,
tender grass,
grass on the rooftops,
blasted by the east wind.

²⁷ But I know your sitting down,
your going out and your coming in,
and your raging against me.
²⁸ Because your raging against me
and your arrogance have reached my ears,
I will put my hook in your nose
and my bit in your mouth;
I will make you go back
the way you came.

²⁹ "This will be the sign for you: This year you will eat what grows on its own, and in the second year what grows from that. But in the third year sow and reap, plant vineyards and eat their fruit. ³⁰ The surviving remnant of the house of Judah will again take root downward and bear fruit upward. ³¹ For a remnant will go out from Jerusalem, and survivors, from Mount Zion. The zeal of the LORD of Armies will accomplish this.

³² Therefore, this is what the LORD says about the king
    of Assyria:
He will not enter this city,
shoot an arrow here,
come before it with a shield,
or build up a siege ramp against it.
³³ He will go back
the way he came,
and he will not enter this city.

This is the LORD's declaration.

³⁴ I will defend this city and rescue it
for my sake and for the sake of my servant David."

DEFEAT AND DEATH OF SENNACHERIB

³⁵ That night the angel of the LORD went out and struck down one hundred eighty-five thousand in the camp of the Assyrians. When the people got up the next morning—there were all the dead bodies! ³⁶ So King Sennacherib of Assyria broke camp and left. He returned home and lived in Nineveh.

³⁷ One day, while he was worshiping in the temple of his god Nisroch, his sons Adrammelech and Sharezer struck him down with the sword and escaped to the land of Ararat. Then his son Esar-haddon became king in his place.

Numbers 21:4-9
THE BRONZE SNAKE

⁴ Then they set out from Mount Hor by way of the Red Sea to bypass the land of Edom, but the people became impatient because of the journey. ⁵ The people spoke against God and Moses: "Why have you led us up from Egypt to die in the wilderness? There is no bread or water, and we detest this wretched food!" ⁶ Then the LORD sent poisonous snakes among the people, and they bit them so that many Israelites died.

⁷ The people then came to Moses and said, "We have sinned by speaking against the Lᴏʀᴅ and against you. Intercede with the Lᴏʀᴅ so that he will take the snakes away from us." And Moses interceded for the people.

⁸ Then the Lᴏʀᴅ said to Moses, "Make a snake image and mount it on a pole. When anyone who is bitten looks at it, he will recover." ⁹ So Moses made a bronze snake and mounted it on a pole. Whenever someone was bitten, and he looked at the bronze snake, he recovered.

Isaiah 9:6–7

⁶ For a child will be born for us,
a son will be given to us,
and the government will be on his shoulders.
He will be named
Wonderful Counselor, Mighty God,
Eternal Father, Prince of Peace.
⁷ The dominion will be vast,
and its prosperity will never end.
He will reign on the throne of David
and over his kingdom,
to establish and sustain it
with justice and righteousness from now on and forever.
The zeal of the Lᴏʀᴅ of Armies will accomplish this.

The End of Hezekiah's Reign

2 Kings 20

HEZEKIAH'S ILLNESS AND RECOVERY

¹ In those days Hezekiah became terminally ill. The prophet Isaiah son of Amoz came and said to him, "This is what the LORD says: 'Set your house in order, for you are about to die; you will not recover.'"

² Then Hezekiah turned his face to the wall and prayed to the LORD, ³ "Please, LORD, remember how I have walked before you faithfully and wholeheartedly and have done what pleases you." And Hezekiah wept bitterly.

⁴ Isaiah had not yet gone out of the inner courtyard when the word of the LORD came to him: ⁵ "Go back and tell Hezekiah, the leader of my people, 'This is what the LORD God of your ancestor David says: I have heard your prayer; I have seen your tears. Look, I will heal you. On the third day from now you will go up to the LORD's temple. ⁶ I will add fifteen years to your life. I will rescue you and this city from the grasp of the king of Assyria. I will defend this city for my sake and for the sake of my servant David.'"

⁷ Then Isaiah said, "Bring a lump of pressed figs." So they brought it and applied it to his infected skin, and he recovered.

⁸ Hezekiah had asked Isaiah, "What is the sign that the LORD will heal me and that I will go up to the LORD's temple on the third day?"

⁹ Isaiah said, "This is the sign to you from the LORD that he will do what he has promised: Should the shadow go ahead ten steps or go back ten steps?"

¹⁰ Then Hezekiah answered, "It's easy for the shadow to lengthen ten steps. No, let the shadow go back ten steps." ¹¹ So the prophet Isaiah called out to the LORD, and he brought the shadow back the ten steps it had descended on the stairway of Ahaz.

HEZEKIAH'S FOLLY

¹² At that time **Merodach-baladan** son of Baladan, king of Babylon, sent letters and a gift to Hezekiah since he heard that he had been sick. ¹³ Hezekiah listened to the letters and showed the envoys his whole treasure house—the silver, the gold, the spices, and the precious oil—and his armory, and everything that was found in his treasuries. There was nothing in his palace and in all his realm that Hezekiah did not show them.

¹⁴ Then the prophet Isaiah came to King Hezekiah and asked him, "Where did these men come from and what did they say to you?"

Hezekiah replied, "They came from a distant country, from Babylon."

[15] Isaiah asked, "What have they seen in your palace?"

Hezekiah answered, "They have seen everything in my palace. There isn't anything in my treasuries that I didn't show them."

[16] Then Isaiah said to Hezekiah, "Hear the word of the LORD: [17] 'Look, the days are coming when everything in your palace and all that your fathers have stored up until today will be carried off to Babylon; nothing will be left,' says the LORD. [18] 'Some of your descendants—who come from you, whom you father—will be taken away, and they will become eunuchs in the palace of the king of Babylon.'"

[19] Then Hezekiah said to Isaiah, "The word of the LORD that you have spoken is good," for he thought: Why not, if there will be peace and security during my lifetime?

HEZEKIAH'S DEATH

[20] The rest of the events of Hezekiah's reign, along with all his might and how he made the pool and the tunnel and brought water into the city, are written in the Historical Record of Judah's Kings. [21] Hezekiah rested with his fathers, and his son Manasseh became king in his place.

2 Kings 21

JUDAH'S KING MANASSEH

[1] Manasseh was twelve years old when he became king, and he reigned fifty-five years in Jerusalem. His mother's name was Hephzibah. [2] He did what was evil in the LORD's sight, imitating the detestable practices of the nations that the LORD had dispossessed before the Israelites. [3] He rebuilt the high places that his father Hezekiah had destroyed and reestablished the altars for Baal. He made an Asherah, as King Ahab of Israel had done; he also bowed in worship to all the stars in the sky and served them. [4] He built altars in the LORD's temple, where the LORD had said, "Jerusalem is where I will put my name." [5] He built altars to all the stars in the sky in both courtyards of the LORD's temple. [6] He sacrificed his son in the fire, practiced witchcraft and divination, and consulted mediums and spiritists. He did a huge amount of evil in the LORD's sight, angering him.

[7] Manasseh set up the carved image of Asherah, which he made, in the temple that the LORD had spoken about to David and his son Solomon: "I will establish my name forever in this temple and in Jerusalem, which I have chosen out of all the tribes of Israel. [8] I will never again cause the feet of the Israelites to wander from the land I gave to their ancestors if only they will be careful to do all I have commanded them—the whole law that my servant Moses commanded them." [9] But they did not listen; Manasseh caused them to stray so that they did worse evil than the nations the LORD had destroyed before the Israelites.

[10] The LORD said through his servants the prophets, [11] "Since King Manasseh of Judah has committed all these detestable acts—worse evil than the Amorites who preceded him had done—and by means of his idols has also caused Judah to sin, [12] this is what the LORD God of Israel says: 'I am about to bring such disaster on Jerusalem and Judah that everyone who hears about it will shudder. [13] I will stretch over Jerusalem the measuring line used on Samaria and the mason's level used on the house of Ahab, and I will wipe Jerusalem clean as one wipes a bowl—wiping it and turning it upside down. [14] I will abandon the remnant of my inheritance and hand them over to their enemies. They will become plunder and spoil to all their enemies, [15] because they have done what is evil in my sight and have angered me from the day their ancestors came out of Egypt until today.'"

[16] Manasseh also shed so much innocent blood that he filled Jerusalem with it from one end to another. This was in addition to his sin that he caused Judah to commit, so that they did what was evil in the LORD's sight.

MANASSEH'S DEATH

[17] The rest of the events of Manasseh's reign, along with all his accomplishments and the sin that he committed, are written in the Historical Record of Judah's Kings. [18] Manasseh rested

with his fathers and was buried in the garden of his own house, the garden of Uzza. His son Amon became king in his place.

[19] Amon was twenty-two years old when he became king, and he reigned two years in Jerusalem. His mother's name was Meshullemeth daughter of Haruz; she was from Jotbah. [20] He did what was evil in the LORD's sight, just as his father Manasseh had done. [21] He walked in all the ways his father had walked; he served the idols his father had served, and he bowed in worship to them. [22] He abandoned the LORD God of his ancestors and did not walk in the ways of the LORD.

[23] Amon's servants conspired against him and put the king to death in his own house. [24] The common people killed all who had conspired against King Amon, and they made his son Josiah king in his place.

[25] The rest of the events of Amon's reign, along with his accomplishments, are written in the Historical Record of Judah's Kings. [26] He was buried in his tomb in the garden of Uzza, and his son Josiah became king in his place.

Proverbs 11:2

When arrogance comes, disgrace follows,
but with humility comes wisdom.

John 14:13–14

[13] "Whatever you ask in my name, I will do it so that the Father may be glorified in the Son. [14] If you ask me anything in my name, I will do it."

150   I & 2 KINGS: OUR GOD REIGNS

NOTES

"*This is what the* Lord *God of your ancestor David says: I have heard your prayer;*
I have seen your tears…"

2 KINGS 20:5

Covenant Renewal

JUDAH'S KING JOSIAH

¹ Josiah was eight years old when he became king, and he reigned thirty-one years in Jerusalem. His mother's name was Jedidah the daughter of Adaiah; she was from Bozkath. ² He did what was right in the LORD's sight and walked in all the ways of his ancestor David; he did not turn to the right or the left.

JOSIAH REPAIRS THE TEMPLE

³ In the eighteenth year of King Josiah, the king sent the court secretary Shaphan son of Azaliah, son of Meshullam, to the LORD's temple, saying, ⁴ "Go up to the high priest Hilkiah so that he may total up the silver brought into the LORD's temple—the silver the doorkeepers have collected from the people. ⁵ It is to be given to those doing the work—those who oversee the Lord's temple. They in turn are to give it to the workmen in the LORD's temple to repair the damage. ⁶ They are to give it to the carpenters, builders, and masons to buy timber and quarried stone to repair the temple. ⁷ But no accounting is to be required from them for the silver given to them since they work with integrity."

THE BOOK OF THE LAW FOUND

⁸ The high priest Hilkiah told the court secretary Shaphan, "I have found the book of the law in the LORD's temple," and he gave the book to Shaphan, who read it.

⁹ Then the court secretary Shaphan went to the king and reported, "Your servants have emptied out the silver that was found in the temple and have given it to those doing the work—those who oversee the LORD's temple." ¹⁰ Then the court secretary Shaphan told the king, "The priest Hilkiah has given me a book," and Shaphan read it in the presence of the king.

¹¹ When the king heard the words of the book of the law, he tore his clothes. ¹² Then he commanded the priest Hilkiah, Ahikam son of Shaphan, Achbor son of Micaiah, the court secretary Shaphan, and the king's servant Asaiah: ¹³ "Go and inquire of the LORD for me, the people, and all Judah about the words in this book that has been found. For great is the LORD's wrath that is kindled against us because our ancestors have not obeyed the words of this book in order to do everything written about us."

HULDAH'S PROPHECY OF JUDGMENT

¹⁴ So the priest Hilkiah, Ahikam, Achbor, Shaphan, and Asaiah went to the prophetess Huldah, wife of Shallum son of Tikvah, son of Harhas, keeper of the wardrobe. She lived in Jerusalem in the Second District. They spoke with her.

DAY

2
5

Josiah, Jehoahaz, Jehoiakim

Judah

15 She said to them, "This is what the LORD God of Israel says: Say to the man who sent you to me, 16 'This is what the LORD says: I am about to bring disaster on this place and on its inhabitants, fulfilling all the words of the book that the king of Judah has read, 17 because they have abandoned me and burned incense to other gods in order to anger me with all the work of their hands. My wrath will be kindled against this place, and it will not be quenched.' 18 Say this to the king of Judah who sent you to inquire of the LORD: 'This is what the LORD God of Israel says: As for the words that you heard, 19 because your heart was tender and you humbled yourself before the LORD when you heard what I spoke against this place and against its inhabitants, that they would become a desolation and a curse, and because you have torn your clothes and wept before me, I myself have heard'—this is the LORD's declaration. 20 'Therefore, I will indeed gather you to your fathers, and you will be gathered to your grave in peace. Your eyes will not see all the disaster that I am bringing on this place.'"

Then they reported to the king.

2 Kings 23

COVENANT RENEWAL

1 So the king sent messengers, and they gathered all the elders of Judah and Jerusalem to him. 2 Then the king went to the LORD's temple with all the men of Judah and all the inhabitants of Jerusalem, as well as the priests and the prophets—all the people from the youngest to the oldest. He read in their hearing all the words of the book of the covenant that had been found in the LORD's temple. 3 Next, the king stood by the pillar and made a covenant in the LORD's presence to follow the LORD and to keep his commands, his decrees, and his statutes with all his heart and with all his soul in order to carry out the words of this covenant that were written in this book; all the people agreed to the covenant.

JOSIAH'S REFORMS

4 Then the king commanded the high priest Hilkiah and the priests of the second rank and the doorkeepers to bring out of the LORD's sanctuary all the articles made for Baal, Asherah, and all the stars in the sky. He burned them outside Jerusalem in the fields of the Kidron and carried their ashes to Bethel. 5 Then he did away with the idolatrous priests the kings of Judah had appointed to burn incense at the high places in the cities of Judah and in the areas surrounding Jerusalem. They had burned incense to Baal, and to the sun, moon, constellations, and all the stars in the sky. 6 He brought out the Asherah pole from the LORD's temple to the Kidron Valley outside Jerusalem. He burned it at the Kidron Valley, beat it to dust, and threw its dust on the graves of the common people. 7 He also tore down the houses of the male cult prostitutes that were in the LORD's temple, in which the women were weaving tapestries for Asherah.

8 Then Josiah brought all the priests from the cities of Judah, and he defiled the high places from Geba to Beer-sheba, where the priests had burned incense. He tore down the high places of the city gates at the entrance of the gate of Joshua the governor of the city (on the left at the city gate). 9 The priests of the high places, however, did not come up to the altar of the LORD in Jerusalem; instead, they ate unleavened bread with their fellow priests.

10 He defiled Topheth, which is in Ben Hinnom Valley, so that no one could sacrifice his son or daughter in the fire to **Molech**. 11 He did away with the horses that the kings of Judah had dedicated to the sun. They had been at the entrance of the LORD's temple in the precincts by the chamber of Nathan-melech, the eunuch. He also burned the chariots of the sun.

12 The king tore down the altars that the kings of Judah had made on the roof of Ahaz's upper chamber. He also tore down the altars that Manasseh had made in the two courtyards of the LORD's temple. Then he smashed them there and threw their dust into the Kidron Valley. 13 The king also defiled the high places that were across from Jerusalem, to the south of the Mount of Destruction, which King Solomon of Israel had built for Ashtoreth, the abhorrent idol of the Sidonians; for Chemosh, the abhorrent idol of Moab; and for Milcom, the detestable idol of the Ammonites. 14 He broke the sacred pillars into pieces, cut down the Asherah poles, then filled their places with human bones.

[15] He even tore down the altar at Bethel and the high place that had been made by Jeroboam son of Nebat, who caused Israel to sin. He burned the high place, crushed it to dust, and burned the Asherah. [16] As Josiah turned, he saw the tombs there on the mountain. He sent someone to take the bones out of the tombs, and he burned them on the altar. He defiled it according to the word of the LORD proclaimed by the man of God who proclaimed these things. [17] Then he said, "What is this monument I see?"

The men of the city told him, "It is the tomb of the man of God who came from Judah and proclaimed these things that you have done to the altar at Bethel."

[18] So he said, "Let him rest. Don't let anyone disturb his bones." So they left his bones undisturbed with the bones of the prophet who came from Samaria.

[19] Josiah also removed all the shrines of the high places that were in the cities of Samaria, which the kings of Israel had made to anger the LORD. Josiah did the same things to them that he had done at Bethel. [20] He slaughtered on the altars all the priests of those high places, and he burned human bones on the altars. Then he returned to Jerusalem.

PASSOVER OBSERVED

[21] The king commanded all the people, "Observe the Passover of the LORD your God as written in the book of the covenant." [22] No such Passover had ever been observed from the time of the judges who judged Israel through the entire time of the kings of Israel and Judah. [23] But in the eighteenth year of King Josiah, the LORD's Passover was observed in Jerusalem.

FURTHER ZEAL FOR THE LORD

[24] In addition, Josiah eradicated the mediums, the spiritists, household idols, images, and all the abhorrent things that were seen in the land of Judah and in Jerusalem. He did this in order to carry out the words of the law that were written in the book that the priest Hilkiah found in the LORD's temple. [25] Before him there was no king like him who turned to the LORD with all his heart and with all his soul and with all his strength according to all the law of Moses, and no one like him arose after him.

[26] In spite of all that, the LORD did not turn from the fury of his intense burning anger, which burned against Judah because of all the affronts with which Manasseh had angered him. [27] For the LORD had said, "I will also remove Judah from my presence just as I have removed Israel. I will reject this city Jerusalem, that I have chosen, and the temple about which I said, 'My name will be there.'"

[28] The rest of the events of Josiah's reign, along with all his accomplishments, are written in the Historical Record of Judah's Kings. [29] During his reign, **Pharaoh Neco** king of Egypt marched up to help the king of Assyria at the Euphrates River. King Josiah went to confront him, and at Megiddo when Neco saw him he killed him. [30] From Megiddo his servants carried his dead body in a chariot, brought him into Jerusalem, and buried him in his own tomb. Then the common people took Jehoahaz son of Josiah, anointed him, and made him king in place of his father.

JUDAH'S KING JEHOAHAZ

[31] Jehoahaz was twenty-three years old when he became king, and he reigned three months in Jerusalem. His mother's name was Hamutal daughter of Jeremiah; she was from Libnah. [32] He did what was evil in the LORD's sight just as his ancestors had done. [33] Pharaoh Neco imprisoned him at Riblah in the land of Hamath to keep him from reigning in Jerusalem, and he imposed on the land a fine of seventy-five hundred pounds of silver and seventy-five pounds of gold.

JUDAH'S KING JEHOIAKIM

[34] Then Pharaoh Neco made Eliakim son of Josiah king in place of his father Josiah and changed Eliakim's name to Jehoiakim. But Neco took Jehoahaz and went to Egypt, and he died there. [35] So Jehoiakim gave the silver and the gold to Pharaoh, but at Pharaoh's command he taxed the land to give it. He exacted the silver and the gold from the common people, each according to his assessment, to give it to Pharaoh Neco.

[36] Jehoiakim was twenty-five years old when he became king, and he reigned eleven years in Jerusalem. His mother's name was Zebidah daughter of Pedaiah; she was from Rumah. [37] He did what was evil in the LORD's sight just as his ancestors had done.

2 Corinthians 5:21

He made the one who did not know sin to be sin for us, so that in him we might become the righteousness of God.

Galatians 3:13–14

[13] Christ redeemed us from the curse of the law by becoming a curse for us, because it is written, Cursed is everyone who is hung on a tree. [14] The purpose was that the blessing of Abraham would come to the Gentiles by Christ Jesus, so that we could receive the promised Spirit through faith.

NOTES

*He did what was right in the L*ORD*'s sight and walked in all the ways of his ancestor David.*

2 KINGS 22:2

Jerusalem Destroyed

2 Kings 24

JEHOIAKIM'S REBELLION AND DEATH

¹ During Jehoiakim's reign, **King Nebuchadnezzar** of Babylon attacked. Jehoiakim became his vassal for three years, and then he turned and rebelled against him. ² The Lord sent Chaldean, Aramean, Moabite, and Ammonite raiders against Jehoiakim. He sent them against Judah to destroy it, according to the word of the LORD he had spoken through his servants the prophets. ³ Indeed, this happened to Judah at the LORD's command to remove them from his presence. It was because of the sins of Manasseh, according to all he had done, ⁴ and also because of all the innocent blood he had shed. He had filled Jerusalem with innocent blood, and the LORD was not willing to forgive.

⁵ The rest of the events of Jehoiakim's reign, along with all his accomplishments, are written in the Historical Record of Judah's Kings. ⁶ Jehoiakim rested with his fathers, and his son Jehoiachin became king in his place.

⁷ Now the king of Egypt did not march out of his land again, for the king of Babylon took everything that had belonged to the king of Egypt, from the Brook of Egypt to the Euphrates River.

JUDAH'S KING JEHOIACHIN

⁸ Jehoiachin was eighteen years old when he became king, and he reigned three months in Jerusalem. His mother's name was Nehushta daughter of Elnathan; she was from Jerusalem. ⁹ He did what was evil in the LORD's sight just as his father had done.

DEPORTATIONS TO BABYLON

¹⁰ At that time the servants of King Nebuchadnezzar of Babylon marched up to Jerusalem, and the city came under siege. ¹¹ King Nebuchadnezzar of Babylon came to the city while his servants were besieging it. ¹² King Jehoiachin of Judah, along with his mother, his servants, his commanders, and his officials, surrendered to the king of Babylon.

So the king of Babylon took him captive in the eighth year of his reign. ¹³ He also carried off from there all the treasures of the LORD's temple and the treasures of the king's palace, and he cut into pieces all the gold articles that King Solomon of Israel had made for the LORD's sanctuary, just as the LORD had predicted. ¹⁴ He deported all Jerusalem and all the commanders and all the best soldiers—ten thousand captives including all the craftsmen and metalsmiths. Except for the poorest people of the land, no one remained.

15 Nebuchadnezzar deported Jehoiachin to Babylon. He took the king's mother, the king's wives, his officials, and the leading men of the land into exile from Jerusalem to Babylon. 16 The king of Babylon brought captive into Babylon all seven thousand of the best soldiers and one thousand craftsmen and metalsmiths—all strong and fit for war. 17 And the king of Babylon made Mattaniah, Jehoiachin's uncle, king in his place and changed his name to Zedekiah.

JUDAH'S KING ZEDEKIAH

18 Zedekiah was twenty-one years old when he became king, and he reigned eleven years in Jerusalem. His mother's name was Hamutal daughter of Jeremiah; she was from Libnah. 19 Zedekiah did what was evil in the LORD's sight just as Jehoiakim had done. 20 Because of the LORD's anger, it came to the point in Jerusalem and Judah that he finally banished them from his presence. Then Zedekiah rebelled against the king of Babylon.

2 Kings 25

NEBUCHADNEZZAR'S SIEGE OF JERUSALEM

1 In the ninth year of Zedekiah's reign, on the tenth day of the tenth month, King Nebuchadnezzar of Babylon advanced against Jerusalem with his entire army. They laid siege to the city and built a siege wall against it all around. 2 The city was under siege until King Zedekiah's eleventh year.

3 By the ninth day of the fourth month the famine was so severe in the city that the common people had no food. 4 Then the city was broken into, and all the warriors fled at night by way of the city gate between the two walls near the king's garden, even though the Chaldeans surrounded the city. As the king made his way along the route to the Arabah, 5 the Chaldean army pursued him and overtook him in the plains of Jericho. Zedekiah's entire army left him and scattered. 6 The Chaldeans seized the king and brought him up to the king of Babylon at Riblah, and they passed sentence on him. 7 They slaughtered Zedekiah's sons before his eyes. Finally, the king of Babylon blinded Zedekiah, bound him in bronze chains, and took him to Babylon.

JERUSALEM DESTROYED

8 On the seventh day of the fifth month—which was the nineteenth year of King Nebuchadnezzar of Babylon— Nebuzaradan, the captain of the guards, a servant of the king of Babylon, entered Jerusalem. 9 He burned the LORD's temple, the king's palace, and all the houses of Jerusalem; he burned down all the great houses. 10 The whole Chaldean army with the captain of the guards tore down the walls surrounding Jerusalem. 11 Nebuzaradan, the captain of the guards, deported the rest of the people who remained in the city, the deserters who had defected to the king of Babylon, and the rest of the population. 12 But the captain of the guards left some of the poorest of the land to be vinedressers and farmers.

13 Now the Chaldeans broke into pieces the bronze pillars of the LORD's temple, the water carts, and the bronze basin, which were in the LORD's temple, and carried the bronze to Babylon. 14 They also took the pots, shovels, wick trimmers, dishes, and all the bronze articles used in the priests' service. 15 The captain of the guards took away the firepans and sprinkling basins—whatever was gold or silver.

16 As for the two pillars, the one basin, and the water carts that Solomon had made for the LORD's temple, the weight of the bronze of all these articles was beyond measure. 17 One pillar was twenty-seven feet tall and had a bronze capital on top of it. The capital, encircled by a grating and pomegranates of bronze, stood five feet high. The second pillar was the same, with its own grating.

18 The captain of the guards also took away Seraiah the chief priest, Zephaniah the priest of the second rank, and the three doorkeepers. 19 From the city he took a court official who had been appointed over the warriors; five trusted royal aides found in the city; the secretary of the commander of the army, who enlisted the people of the land for military duty; and sixty men from the common people who were found within the city. 20 Nebuzaradan, the captain of the guards, took them and brought them to the king of Babylon at Riblah. 21 The king of Babylon put them to death at Riblah in the land of Hamath. So Judah went into exile from its land.

GEDALIAH MADE GOVERNOR

22 King Nebuchadnezzar of Babylon appointed Gedaliah son of Ahikam, son of Shaphan, over the rest of the people he left in the land of Judah. 23 When all the commanders of the armies—they and their men—heard that the king

of Babylon had appointed Gedaliah, they came to Gedaliah at Mizpah. The commanders included Ishmael son of Nethaniah, Johanan son of Kareah, Seraiah son of Tanhumeth the Netophathite, and Jaazaniah son of the Maacathite—they and their men. ²⁴ Gedaliah swore an oath to them and their men, assuring them, "Don't be afraid of the servants of the Chaldeans. Live in the land and serve the king of Babylon, and it will go well for you."

²⁵ In the seventh month, however, Ishmael son of Nethaniah, son of Elishama, of the royal family, came with ten men and struck down Gedaliah, and he died. Also, they killed the Judeans and the Chaldeans who were with him at Mizpah. ²⁶ Then all the people, from the youngest to the oldest, and the commanders of the army, left and went to Egypt, for they were afraid of the Chaldeans.

JEHOIACHIN PARDONED

²⁷ On the twenty-seventh day of the twelfth month of the thirty-seventh year of the exile of Judah's King Jehoiachin, in the year **Evil-merodach** became king of Babylon, he pardoned King Jehoiachin of Judah and released him from prison. ²⁸ He spoke kindly to him and set his throne over the thrones of the kings who were with him in Babylon. ²⁹ So Jehoiachin changed his prison clothes, and he dined regularly in the presence of the king of Babylon for the rest of his life. ³⁰ As for his allowance, a regular allowance was given to him by the king, a portion for each day, for the rest of his life.

Joshua 5:10–12

FOOD FROM THE LAND

¹⁰ While the Israelites camped at Gilgal on the plains of Jericho, they observed the Passover on the evening of the fourteenth day of the month. ¹¹ The day after Passover they ate unleavened bread and roasted grain from the produce of the land. ¹² And the day after they ate from the produce of the land, the manna ceased. Since there was no more manna for the Israelites, they ate from the crops of the land of Canaan that year.

John 2:19–22

¹⁹ Jesus answered, "Destroy this temple, and I will raise it up in three days."

²⁰ Therefore the Jews said, "This temple took forty-six years to build, and will you raise it up in three days?"

²¹ But he was speaking about the temple of his body. ²² So when he was raised from the dead, his disciples remembered that he had said this, and they believed the Scripture and the statement Jesus had made.

NOTES

So Judah went into exile from its land.

2 KINGS 25:21

Grace Day

DAY 27   Use this day to pray, rest, and reflect on this week's
         reading, giving thanks for the grace that is ours in Christ.

He made the one who did not
know sin to be sin for us, so that
in him we might become the
righteousness of God.

2 CORINTHIANS 5:21

DATE ....

W
E
E
K
L
Y

DAY · · · 28

T
R
U
T
H

Scripture is God-breathed and true. When we memorize it, we carry the gospel with us wherever we go.

This week we will memorize a verse from God's reply to King Hezekiah through the prophet Isaiah in Day 23, a reminder that God is intimately involved in the lives of His people.

Find the corresponding memory card in the back of this book.

"But I know your sitting down, your going out and your coming in, and your raging against me."

2 KINGS 19:27

DOWNLOAD THE APP

STOP BY
shereadstruth.com

SHOP
shopshereadstruth.com

SEND A NOTE
hello@shereadstruth.com

SHARE
#SheReadsTruth

BIBLIOGRAPHY

Barry, John D., David Bomar, Derek R. Brown, Rachel Klippenstein, Douglas Mangum, Carrie Sinclair Wolcott, Lazarus Wentz, Elliot Ritzema, and Wendy Widder, eds. *The Lexham Bible Dictionary*. Bellingham, WA: Lexham Press, 2016.

Freedman, David Noel, Allen C. Myers, and Astrid B. Beck. *Eerdmans Dictionary of the Bible*. Grand Rapids, MI: W.B. Eerdmans, 2000.

SHE READS TRUTH *is a worldwide community of women who read God's Word together every day.*

Founded in 2012, She Reads Truth invites women of all ages to engage with Scripture through daily reading plans, online conversation led by a vibrant community of contributors, and offline resources created at the intersection of beauty, goodness, and Truth.

FOR THE RECORD

WHERE DID I STUDY?

O HOME
O OFFICE
O COFFEE SHOP
O CHURCH
O A FRIEND'S HOUSE
O OTHER

WHAT WAS I LISTENING TO?

ARTIST:

SONG:

PLAYLIST:

WHEN DID I STUDY?

MORNING

AFTERNOON

NIGHT

What did I learn?

WHAT WAS HAPPENING IN MY LIFE?

WHAT WAS HAPPENING IN THE WORLD?

| MONTH | DAY | YEAR |

END DATE